NEVER

SPANK A PORCUPINE

Tales From an Old Vermont
Farmwife Who *Did*

Phyllis Tenney Mudgett

*Some chapters are re-published with permission from The Herald of Randolph (Vt) and The Green Mountain Trading Post (Vt).

A WORD FROM AN OLD VERMONT FARMWIFE

I have spanked a number of porcupines in my lifetime, although only one literally. This is a collection of accounts of occasions when I have said: "Someday I'm going to laugh about this!"

I never get up in the morning and say: "What outrageous thing can I do today?"

Things happen, and I cope. Honest..

CONTENTS

PROLOGUE

It's appropriate to begin at the end, I guess. It is a scene that has been written all too often during the past few decades in Vermont, and on dairy farms all over the country. Farmers must retire. Their children have seen the farms on which they have grown up and worked so hard with their parents become less profitable and more financially stressed year by year. Seeing no future in dairying, they have taken up other occupations and, as sad as it is for them to see the farm and lands they love become one more city buyer's "gentleman's farm," they know they don't want to spend their lives struggling in a lost cause.

So Merl and I take one last look through the now empty farmhouse where Merl grew up, where we spent our first year of marriage, where we raised our four daughters, and leave with tears in our eyes, to go and sign the papers that will transfer it to a young couple who plan to grow organic vegetables.

There are no crops on the farm this year, other than a few fields of run-out hay. Two neighboring farmers who utilized our river bottom corn ground after Merl quit milking cows ten years ago have gone out of business. The farmer who grew corn here last year drove twenty miles to do it, and decided that it isn't practical. So those beautiful fields that once held such lush stands of alfalfa and fodder corn, now lie in corn stubble and weeds. Merl was showing the boundaries of a field to the buyer, who remarked:

"That is really a heavy stand of witch grass!"

"It's crab grass," said Merl.

We hope the buyers aren't planning to live on gardening profits from the start.

So, from a shaky beginning, when we left Merl's boyhood farm over a serious dispute with his parents, with the severe asthma I had developed at age fifteen that hospitalized me every few weeks on the verge of death; to a rented farm down the road a couple of years later with a fistful of debt and just four baby calves to start our herd; with my doing the milking and feeding, the plowing and harrowing, planting and mowing, raking and baling; with my two babies playing around me in the stable, or in a shady corner of the field where I was working; with Merl toiling at a factory forty miles away, nine hours every night, then putting down silage for me, and cleaning stables, and throwing bales, and setting fence posts, and doing all the other heavy work, when he should have been sleeping; through numerous jobs for both of us over the years; to buying the home farm from his sister in 1960 and deciding that either the cows could support us now, or we'd be done with them (brave words he never could bring himself to follow through on, until forced to by his failing health); with Terry and Diane coming three years apart, then Lisa nine years later, and, when we had almost despaired of having more children, our little bonus, Tracy, five years after that; with successes and failures, adventures and misadventures, Merl and I now face a new life once again, eagerly, happily on our own.

NEWBORN CALF

Phyllis Tenney Mudgett

Ah, joy! You're a heifer,
You beautiful mite,
So sleek and shiny,
Healthy and bright,
Straight sturdy back,
Legs straight and strong,
Wide forehead, nice markings,
Fine pedigree long.
You're a bit of perfection,
My treasure, I think
I'll shove your head
Through this bucket,
If you don't learn to drink!

———————————

Published in a 1959 edition of

American Agriculturist

COWS, KIDS, AND OTHER INCURABLE AFFLICTIONS

There's a lot to be said for dairy farming, I keep telling myself. Actually, dairying wouldn't be bad at all if it weren't for cows. Now no one should infer from this that I don't like cows. I do. I really do, especially with onions, mushrooms, and gravy.

My writers' conference faculty advisor held in his hand the two chapters of a book proposal I had submitted.

"I don't find out for the first three paragraphs who you are," he complained. "You need to start right off by saying that you're a thirty-three year old housewife from the Bronx, that you and your husband got fed up with city life, so you loaded your two dogs into your Volkswagen and moved to Vermont, and you didn't know a thing about farming....!"

"But I still live in the Vermont town I was born in, my family was there when the Indians burned it in 1780, I was milking cows by hand when I was ten, and if there's anything I know about, it's farming!"

I felt like a pinned insect specimen under his intense scrutiny.

"I never heard of anyone like that writing a book," he said.

I can't say his reaction to my background was the reason for setting aside my book writing for so long, but I'm here to tell him now, many years later, that it's high time he did hear of one.

As I said before, there's a lot to be said for dairy farming. And it really wouldn't be bad if it weren't for cows. Now, before I start getting wrathful letters from offended cow lovers—not dairymen, or especially dairy women, they'll know exactly what I'm talking about—but the kind of cow lovers who buy plywood cow cutouts for their yards, and cow potholders for their kitchens, and never have to shovel into a cow, or shovel away from her, or put up with all her contrariness and quirks in between, let me impart a little basic information about cows.

If you're a dairyman, you're not running a milk factory. You are operating a perpetual maternity ward full of pregnant, very pregnant, or about to become pregnant, lactating (for the most part) females, with all the hormonal fluctuations and temperament changes that implies.

A cow has four stomachs. She would have you believe she is extremely picky about what goes into them. She will turn her nose up at perfect third-cutting alfalfa hay, if she can stretch her neck five feet to steal grain from the higher producing cow beside her. Yet she will swallow anything that will fit through her mouth when you aren't looking. I once caught a cow that had slipped through the electric fence and come back to the barn happily licking up a pailful of shingle nails from the repair job beside the heifer shed. Shingle nails, wire, and scrap metal don't do those four stomachs any appreciable good.

Dairymen keep the magnet makers of the world in Mercedes sedans. You shoot a large smooth magnet down the cow's gullet with a balling gun, in the hopes that the metals she has ingested, intentionally or otherwise, will cluster on the magnet and not puncture anything vital until the stomach acids can dispose of them. Sometimes it works. Sometimes you put in another magnet. If your barn had metal walls, you could slap some of the fools up on them for animated fridgies. I have had visions, in my more manic moments, of looking down in the pasture someday, to see the whole herd spinning and darting as their magnetic poles repel each other, and then suddenly snapping together into a cluster, like so many big rusty iron filings. At least then I would know where they all were for once. Aside from eating nails and pieces of fencing wire, drinking kerosene, --ah, yes, on top of the workbench in the tool shed, with some rusty auction wrenches soaking in it! (It was fortunate that the old sot was dry, because, had she been milking, it might have contaminated a whole tankful of milk. We worried that her impromptu drinking spree might abort her calf, but the calf was born healthy to all appearances, and certainly, with no rust on him) and mooching dropped apples, which makes a cow very drunk, and dries off her milk supply completely, and often results in her being sent to that Big Hamburger Stand in the sky, aside from all these, the cow's consuming passion is for being where she isn't.

There are fences that will keep cows where they belong. Rich gentleman farmers and horsey hobby farmers have them built. Working farmers try to maintain secure property line fences, but for sectioning off fields and pastures, they tend to have to rely on electric fences, their families, and the Lord, not necessarily in that order, to keep the cows where they want them.

It helps if you can be philosophical about it. It is not a pretty sight to watch a personality disintegrate because someone can't help taking to heart the fact that a certain cow cannot be contained in an ordinary fence.

We had such a cow when we were first married. We had worked hard to provide a beautiful field of young oats, covering a new seeding of clover and hay grasses, and we proudly turned our little herd into it, anticipating their ecstasy. They didn't disappoint us, burying their pretty little Jersey faces in the lush green. We went off to do a rugged day of fieldwork.

When we came back to bring them in for milking, Bobbie was missing. We found her down the road, munching chokecherry leaves. Aside from the dubious nutrient value of cherry leaves, under certain conditions, they are quite deadly to livestock. We were not happy with her. We went back after chores were done, and checked the entire fence. Everything was in order.

The next morning, when I turned the cows out, I hung around on the knoll above them to watch Bobbie eat her fill of grass. She went over for a drink, looked up at me, then went and laid down. I trudged up to work. She was down the road again when I went after them that night. Again, the fence was intact.

The next day, I moved back out of sight after I had turned them out. Bobbie followed her same routine. I checked at noon, and she was still lying there. At milking time, she was back in the chokecherries.

This was getting serious. We couldn't have her doing that, but I shouldn't waste time that needed to be spent on spring fieldwork. My husband was working off the farm at a full time job, and doing farm work with me at night and on weekends.

"I guess you're just going to have to take a day to watch her, to see how she's getting out," he said.

The next morning, I picked a spot that was hidden from her, and this time I fooled her. She didn't bother to take her morning nap. As soon as she had taken her fill and her drink, she walked over to the fence, put her head under the wire and wriggled through with bowed back, as if the electric current were her personal back-scratcher. I went down and persuaded her, with the help of an intimidating willow switch, to forego her cherry leaves, and to take her stall up in the barn for the rest of the day.

Merl and I talked over what we should do about her. He

vetoed my suggestions. Then he had an idea. We hitched a tie chain around her neck, and attached a short length of chain to the underside of it. When she lowered her head, the chain would drag.

Once again, I spied on her in the morning. She approached the fence with her usual aplomb, and then lowered her head under the wire. It had a remarkable, and, I thought, gratifying, effect. As she pushed underneath, the chain at the top of her neck made contact with the fence, while the length that was dragging made good contact with the dewy ground. The result was impressive. She jumped backward with a loud bellow.

Now I have touched battery operated fences in my day. I did it routinely, with a green blade of grass, to test the battery's strength. And, in my more reckless youth, my brothers, cousins, and I took a perverted delight in coaxing some unsuspecting newcomer to hold on to the last hand in a chain of us, while the first one grasped a live fence, gladly taking the current that ran through us to give the new guy at the end a super jolt. It had been done to me. Once. So I knew just what that cow had experienced, and it wasn't very bad, but she had a tantrum.

She bellowed, she roared, she bucked, and she put her head on the ground and tried to rub the chain off. She was furious. Finally, she went over into the shade and sulked. I went to the tractor, triumphant.

Two days later, all the cows were down the road, and one whole section of fence was down. Merl nearly took the 30-30 rifle to work with him, so I wouldn't put a permanent stop to her. Once again, I lay in wait in the morning.

Bobbie finished grazing, got her drink, walked over to a docile heifer and butted her under the belly hard enough to raise her off her hind legs. The startled heifer recovered her balance and ran out of reach. Bobbie walked over to the next cow and knocked the wind out of her. Soon she had them all nervous and milling in one end of the pasture. Watching her chance, she hooked a small cow under the ribs and threw her right through the fence, taking the wire off two posts. Calmly, she stepped over the wire, with head and chain held high, and started down the road. I ran down to repair the fence before the others followed, then put the old outlaw back in the barn, where she stayed, and had her green feed brought to her, until we moved all the cows back to permanent pasture the next week.

One autumn afternoon, several years later, after we had bought our present farm, our daughters, Terry and Diane, had entered grammar school, and Bobbie was just an anecdote, I looked out to see what was upsetting the dog. Streaming down across the corn-stubbled field was our whole herd of Jerseys, tails over their backs, bucking and jumping like spring calves. I ran toward the car, but then saw that they were making a sweeping turn and were heading back toward the dry lot on my end. I ran down around the barn to discourage them from turning toward the road. I could see their devious minds clicking into gear when they spotted me. Divide and conquer. Half of them swept on by, and the other half whirled toward the river and headed south again.

I wheezed desperately back to the car, left the driveway on two wheels, and sped down the road to cut them off at the pass. They wheeled and ran up the river edge, but now the others were back near the dry lot and were running up around the barn. I flew the quarter mile back up the field, got by them and honked them back to the others.

We ended in an uneasy standoff, with me patrolling the road in the car, and them making half-hearted feints at a getaway, while I waited for my little daughters to get home from school. I hailed them as they got off the bus, and shouted strategic orders like a berserk general.

"Terry, you guard the road up around the barn! Diane, you stand over on the knoll so you can close in and help Terry if you need to! I'll try to work them up toward the pen!"

Terry and Diane took their places, and the cows walked docilely up to the pen and went in. The girls ran down and closed the gate securely.

They told their father about it when he got home from work.

"We put the cows back in for you, Daddy," they said. "Mommy was letting them run all over the field!"

As I mentioned before, there's a lot to be said for dairy farming. With small children around, there's a lot that should probably be left unsaid

.

STARTING OUT

"Poor folks gotta have fun somehow!" my mother exclaimed whenever an impulsive irrational act of friend or relative had us laughing and shaking our heads. I was a teenager before she explained the origin of that expression.

In Tunbridge, Vermont, where my mother grew up, was a family which was visibly struggling to get by, but which was enlarged, year by year, with a new baby.

A neighbor finally voiced what most observers were thinking.

"Ned, you ain't got two nickels to rub together! Why the heck do you keep havin' young ones one after another?"

"Wa-al," said Ned thoughtfully, "we ain't got money to go to the movies, and poor folks gotta have fun somehow."

I was reminded of it that morning, as I vigorously hoed my garden, while I waited for Merl to get dressed, and to calm down enough for it to be safe for me to go back into the kitchen without risking an orange juice shampoo. Now and then I glanced down with a grin at the little trailer we called home, only mildly regretting the delay on our stable-building project.

The start of our dairy farming centered on the neighboring farm that Merl had rented when he was still farming his parents' place. This old farm had a three-story barn with an old overhead wooden cow stable. The owners lived in western Vermont, but retained the house for family visits.

We made a deal with the landlady: we would put in a concrete stable downstairs, and a new milk house, in lieu of rent for five years. Our first task was to remove twenty years of accumulation of manure that been scraped down through trap doors in the stable floor above in years past from beneath the old stable.

By the following spring, we had bought an old manure spreader, plow, rake, and mower with Merl's winter wages, and with his older brother co-signing a $500 note, we got a FarmAll "H" tractor. The tractor was so ancient that it had started its career with iron wheels. Along the way, somebody had modernized it by cutting the spokes and welding on wheels with rubber tires. They hadn't measured exactly, however, and the tractor had a curious rolling gait that gave one the feeling of riding a limping horse down the road. But it would do for now, and our front-end loader fit it.

We were only half joking when we kidded about the barn falling down if we removed the manure. It was piled right up to the floor. There was a mud hole beside the barn and little room to maneuver, so, rather than deal with the mud, and with hitching and unhitching the spreader for each load, we tackled the job by hand. In spite of my asthma, I was very strong, and I swung my four-tine fork beside Merl with his huge silage fork. We loaded the little spreader heaping full each time in five minutes. Then I galumphed away to the fields to spread it, while Merl worked on forms for the milk house foundation. Two-year-old Terry was his sidekick and helper. There was no power at the farm yet, so Merl sawed the pieces by hand. As he put the saw down, Terry took it up, and worked on her own piece of wood. Then he'd need the saw, so he'd take it from her, and put down his hammer. She'd just be started with the hammer when he'd need it again. Finally, she threw down her board in disgust.

"Deepers, Dawdy!"

Her dad was a talented yodeler, and she picked it up as soon as she could talk. Sometimes, when I had backed up the spreader, and shut the tractor off, I could hear the rafters rattling as they yodeled together.

All that fertilizer was a godsend for those worn out fields. By the time we had the pit scraped down to raw dirt, we had our corn and new hay seeding planted, and were ready to start haying.

Building a cow stable is an expensive hobby, and so is eating, so we both took jobs at a supermarket in Hanover, New Hampshire, while Terry spent her days with grandparents. As soon as we got home, I mowed or raked, while Merl, with Terry playing about him, worked on forms for the stable. We hired the baling done that year, and often spent half the night putting in hay, while she slumbered on the front seat of the truck. Then back to Hanover in the morning and repeat. Our eighteen-hour work-days didn't leave much time for home life, but we were exhilarated by what we were accomplishing, and we enjoyed our little girl and each other.

So here we were on this beautiful June day, with our first cutting of hay safely in the barn, our corn cultivated for the second time, and a whole long Saturday of "spare" time to build the stable. Merl was usually champing at the bit to be up and at work, but this morning—of all days—he was goofing off.

I was first to arise. Merl didn't follow me. I was eager to be at our work, so I urged him a time or two to pile out of bed. I put on the bacon, dressed the baby, set the table—and he still wasn't up. I stepped into the bedroom, stirring the pitcher of icy orange juice in my hand.

"It's nearly eight o'clock," I said. "I broke the budget on a great breakfast. Are you going to come out and eat it?"

He grinned, stretched, and clasped his hands behind his head.

"I'll have my breakfast in bed this morning."

"Okay, here's your juice," I said, pouring it on his bare chest, "how'll you have your eggs?"

I was happy that his sense of modesty prevented pursuit out of the door. We accomplished a lot of work on the stable that day. Later.

HERE'S ADVICE, AND ADVICE

The magazine articles of the 1950s, which dispensed copious advice on the care and feeding of babies and husbands, had little relevance for me. It took time, however, for me to learn to ignore them. I had pored over those magazines during my early teen years, and I thought they held the key to becoming the perfect wife and mother. The only problem, after I married at age seventeen, was that their advice never seemed to fit my situation. I found articles on how to tempt a finicky child's appetite. None of them had any counsel for a young mother whose two-year-old ate cow grain every time Mommy turned her back.

"But I'm a calf, Mommy!" Terry protested.

Aside from consideration of the sanitary aspects of licking grain from the manger and drinking from the cow's water bowl, there was another compelling reason why I tried to spoil her fun. Any cow has a strong proprietary interest in her immediate territory. She is likely to regard a child as just another trespassing, ill-mannered dog, and she has a tendency to throw any unwary, trespassing, ill-mannered dog several feet with her head. I didn't think my little daughter would be as agile or resilient as the cow-dog puppy.

Pat, the puppy, never forgot or forgave that treatment. For

all of her adult life (and she lived fifteen years) I would see her sometimes saunter around to the feed walk to lick grain, threatening with bared teeth and throaty growl some perfectly innocent cow, that was forced to hold her nose up, motionless, until Pat, satisfied that she had once more established who was now The Boss, would take a couple of sloppy licks of water from the bowl, and then strut back stiff-legged, with tail belligerently straight out behind her, to take her place again on the back walk where she could supervise my milking. A dog after my own heart.

I soon learned that keeping the romance in marriage on our dairy farm was accomplished a bit differently from any of the methods those city editors and writers might have devised. A straight furrow with plows properly adjusted to turn the sod evenly; avoiding the too sharp turn in silty bottomland soil that would bury the harrows and rear wheels of the tractor; easing the truck or wagon load of hay over bumps without spilling bales or spouse to the ground; mowing fields swiftly and efficiently and not leaving any "manes" of un-cut grass; raking, baling, stacking bales, milking cows, feeding calves, harrowing, planting, ensiling, to the exacting Mudgett specifications…all that kept my husband mellow and attentive, not candlelight dinners. The one candlelight dinner I prepared in the early years was the last I tried for a long time.

I had completed the milking and my share of the feeding chores one weekend evening, and had hurried in to get a special supper on by the time Merl finished up. The table was set with a red-checkered cloth and our wedding china, water goblets and silverware, the baby was snugly asleep in her crib, soft music from the radio, the candles glowing, when Merl came in to wash up. He seated himself at his place, squinted at the chicken pie bubbling through its golden biscuits, the fluffy mashed potatoes, the buttered sliced beets, the tender green asparagus, and the plump raised yeast rolls before him.

"Forget to pay the light bill?" he asked.

None of those other columns I read, as a bride, about learning to cook or keep house, was particularly pertinent, either. We ate a lot of leftovers until I learned to cook for just two.

At home, before marriage, I always took the dishpan to the cellar to fill it with potatoes from the bin for dinner, grabbing two or three quarts of vegetables from the shelves while I was down there. While there were officially only four children in my family, seldom were there fewer than a dozen people or more at our table, as my mother added another leaf, and made up another bed for whichever relative or local old-timer needed a home for a while. And whole families of children, who had been sent from Boston to board with us for the summer while their parents worked at wartime jobs, ended up staying with us year around for years. I learned quantity cooking at a young age, and it took real effort on my part to un-learn what had become second nature to me. In time, I managed.

Some habits, however, I never changed.

My husband's brothers and father helped us put up our corn silage a couple of weeks after we were married. I came in early to put on a hearty dinner for them, topped off with a selection of pies I had baked the night before. They started to laugh when I put the pies on the table. It took a moment for me to realize what they found funny. My crusts were evenly crimped around the edges!

"You'd better enjoy this, Boy, while you can!" they ribbed Merl. "When the babies arrive and the work piles up, you'll be lucky to have pie to say nothing about pie with fancy edges!"

He always had his pie, and to this day, I flute the edges to seal them, just as I did standing on a chair so many years ago, "helping" my grandmother.

The sagacious advice on how to adjust to living with another person in a new marriage fell far short for me, too.

None of it told me, for instance, what to do about a jealous cow dog who couldn't bear to see Merl and me embrace. He had had Merl all to himself before I came along!

He came racing around the stable during one of our playful scuffles one night at milking time, and latched onto the back of my scalp! What really endeared him to me, however, was his little trick of circling around behind, when I took him after cows, to sneak up and nip me on the back of my bare leg. He became less enamored of that stunt when I watched his shadow, and, timing it perfectly, kicked up with my heel to catch him under the chops just as he lunged to bite me. He behaved himself until his sore tongue healed.

I doubt that the fashion writers, who warned brides to never let their husbands see them in hair curlers, could have envisioned the grooming problems I faced as a new bride. I had just climbed off the old horse-drawn corn planter we pulled behind the tractor. It required a person on the planter to raise and lower it, and to monitor its quirky operation. The field was dry, and the dust had coated me from head to foot when my mother drove in one day to take me for a much-needed haircut.

Even my farm-bred, tomboy mother was taken aback at the amount of dirt on me.

"I'll wash up and change…!"

"No, we're running late," she said.

I hurriedly beat the dust off my clothes as best I could, then splashed water on my face, and was about to duck my head under the faucet, when she called:

"Don't bother to rinse your hair. You're going to have a shampoo anyway."

Off we went to the beauty salon. The poor operator was appalled.

"What happened to you?!"

"It's good clean loam," I explained, and was grateful when it didn't clog her sink. It can't be often that a hairdresser sees such a dramatic visible improvement in a client.

As much as those women's magazines fell short on advice for me, they did help me develop a good sense of interior decorating, and I honed my cooking skills on their food sections. And, ultimately, I used them as a mulch base around my perennial flowers and fruit trees. They kept the weeds from coming up for three years or more. It was gratifying to know they weren't a total waste.

.4

WITH LIBERTY FOR ALL…EXCEPT
DAIRYMEN

In all our years of farming, there was only one creamery manager whom I dreaded to see driving into the yard.

When we first started shipping milk to that creamery, there was no problem and our relationship with him was quite congenial. Our barn was usually clean and orderly, heavily bedded with fragrant sawdust, and we had built a huge, first rate milk house on the rented farm, equipped with one of the area's first big stainless steel vacuum bulk milk tanks. This, with a good record of producing rich, high quality Jersey milk should have kept him happy. And it did for quite a while, until, that is, he discovered our personal farming arrangement.

He showed up one night, just as I was changing the milkers onto the last set of cows. I couldn't stop to talk, but he tagged behind me, talking to me, until I had the last of the milkers off and into the milk house, rinsed, and chugging away on the automatic washer. I tugged the dump station and hose into the milk house, and rinsed and washed them.

There was far too much noise in the milk house for me to hear what he was saying, with bulk tank compressor and teat cup washer running full blast, and the dump station hose dryer screaming, but he didn't let that stop him. Glancing at him from time to time, I had the same impression I get watching fish facing me in an aquarium—that they are shouting messages to me on which I should be taking notes. As soon as the teat cup washer cycle was complete, I stopped the hose dryer and threw the switch on the bulk tank, so I could carry on a conversation with him while I scrubbed up the equipment and rinsed down the milk house.

All went well while he inquired casually about how things were going, how much production increase we expected later in the season, whether there were any problems he could help with. Then he asked when Merl would be back.

"About two a.m." I said.

"You mean you're doing chores all alone tonight?"

"I do every night. Merl's working the second shift at Cone Automatic Machine Company in Windsor, with two hours of overtime five days a week."

"Well, what are you doing about haying? Do you have hired help?" he demanded.

"I'm the 'hired help'. I can handle getting the hay cut, raked and baled. We put it in the barn when Merl is home. I try to have a bunch of it ready for the weekends, if the weather cooperates."

I wasn't prepared for his reaction. From a mildly obnoxious man, with an over-bearing swagger, he was suddenly a pacing beast, bristling with pent up rage and indignation.

"You can't farm that way!" he exclaimed. "There's no way--! Well, I wish I could get work done that…! This won't do!"

I watched him, taking in this amazing outburst and digesting it.

He knew our first cutting of hay was all in the barn by June tenth, because I had told him while I was finishing the milking.

And he also knew that we were planning to start our second cutting the twentieth of June. What I knew was that, in addition to being creamery manager, he was also manager of the dairy connected with it, which had served as a rich man's plaything, and as a valued contributor to fine Jersey breeding for decades. I also knew that his large farm crew was nowhere near finished with their first hay cutting, and they were milking a herd no larger than our own.

"It works for us," I said mildly.

"Well," he spluttered, "it won't do! It won't do at all!" and he left in a cloud of dust.

I hastily finished my chores and went in to get supper for my daughters.

When I went into the milk house in the morning and began to turn on the switches, realization hit me like a kick in the stomach. I snatched a lid off the bulk tank, and the stench hit me full in the face. I had turned off the compressor the night before to listen to that chauvinist egotist carry on about my doing our farm work, and I had neglected to turn it back on to cool the night's milk!

I stood there, sickened at the loss of income, and watched a nearly full tank of milk go down the drain, gaining only momentary comfort from a fleeting vision of that ill-tempered creamery manager dog-paddling frantically in the milk as he was swept in concentric swirls into oblivion.

His follow-up visits focused much more on questions about how we accomplished our plowing, planting, cultivating, and harvesting, than on our sanitary conditions, which were excellent. I answered his questions more and more sparingly, since each snippet of information engendered even deeper hostility and more pronounced irritability.

He could see for himself that I was capably milking more than forty cows, that I had two small daughters to care for, a large garden to tend, and that our crops and harvested feed were of excellent quality.

It was driving him crazy.

I couldn't see that it was any of his business, but he calmed down considerably when Merl quit his job at the machine shop. He didn't know about the other two or three part-time jobs Merl was holding down, and I didn't bother to tell him.

Several years later, now on our own farm, with the fall crops all in, our third daughter, Lisa only five weeks old, we were still strapped for funds, and Merl went back to work nights at the factory. A few weeks later, that same creamery manager caught me feeding silage (we were now milking sixty cows, and winter chores took me twelve to fourteen hours a day, depending upon which equipment was frozen or buried in snow) and our dastardly secret was out. He left in a blithering rage.

In a couple of days he was back.

The double soapstone sink in our milk house was no longer regulation. We would have to replace it with stainless steel. I called our supplier and learned that it must be ordered from the distributor.

In a few days my nemesis was back, more bellicose than ever.

"I told you that you had to replace that sink!"

"We are replacing it! Joe's Equipment has ordered it for us. It should be here in two weeks."

"That's not good enough! You're all done shipping milk!"

"You can't do that!" I protested. "We haven't had any problems with our bacteria count or milk quality!"

He could, and he did. He instantly learned that my fury, when fueled by rank injustice, reduced his tantrums to grape-squashing snits. He escaped before I hit him with the bulk tank.

Another company, with a sane creamery manager, began to pick up our milk the next day, but I spent several sleepless nights gnashing my teeth over that first ruthless, power-drunk, self-centered little tyrant, and concocting elaborate schemes for revenge.

He up and died before I could carry any of them out, which I thought was downright unsporting of him. It took me a long time to forgive him for that, too.

TAKING NO PRISONERS

Except for a few rather striking exceptions in my past, I think I'm quite an easy-going person. Coming from a long line of independent Vermonters, I am thoroughly imbued with the philosophy of "live and let live." If the crows stay out of the corn piece, they're perfectly welcome to scold me all they want to when I drive the tractor into the hay field. Not until squirrels sneak into the cow grain or into the attic to gnaw on electric wires do I pop them off with the .22 rifle. And it is only when the woodchucks move down from the alfalfa in the farther end of the field, into my garden, that I declare war.

I have lived with the laughing derision from my daughters, and the puzzled protests of friends, as I trapped a hapless bee or paper wasp in a water glass against the window, then slipped a paper under it to hold them while I took them out onto the porch to free them.

I have even rescued those big beetles that show up from heaven knows where, and end up on their backs in my bathtub, flailing their legs helplessly. I'd hate to incur capital punishment for every stupid thing I ever did.

Yellow jacket wasps, however, are another matter.

My first serious encounter, at age twelve, was when my friend, Tiny, and I were riding our ponies one day, and we turned up onto the bank beside the road to take a shortcut to her house. We had done it often without incident, but this day we rode right by a new yellow jacket nest. We both yelled, as our ankles took fire, and our ponies went frantic. Tiny's pony took flight, but mine went to her knees, and scrubbed the sides of her face on the ground. We avoided that path from then on.

A few years ago, Merl and I were camping for the summer in an RV park on Lake Champlain. The park had no room for our garden, so we scouted around, and found an over-grown field behind the park, up near one of the large expensive houses on the plateau overlooking the lake. We asked the owner if we could rent a garden space for the summer. He said we could use the land for nothing.

We planted a large garden, and it grew beautifully, although Merl lowered the lake level by three feet, trucking water to it. (Well, that's what we told people was the reason for the record low level that year.) We planted a row of bright flowers on the front facing the road, and I put hills of flowers at the end of each different vegetable row. With the assortment of cheerful sunflowers bobbing their heads from the corn rows, it was very attractive. As the vegetables ripened, we often took a bagful over to the owner.

The end of summer came, and we were gathering the last of the vegetables that we were going to take before we turned the remainder over to our daughter, who lived on a dairy farm a few miles away. Merl had taken the pails to the car, and turned it around and drove down the slight bank beside the garden to pick me up. He must have driven over a wasp nest.

At the last minute, I had decided to pick a bouquet of cosmos. I was bent over, when a sharp sting occurred on my rear, right through my jeans. I straightened up, and a furious yellow jacket wasp buzzed in my face, trying to get my eyes.

I rushed to the car, swatting at him, and managed to get the car door shut before he got inside. We drove out the long drive to the main road, then along the lake to the park, and wound our way up to our space in the back. I got out of the car, and the wasp rushed at my eyes again!

I made it to the camper, slapping him off, and through the door. He wasn't giving up. I picked up a can of Yard Guard and let him have it. It took four solid squirts before he backed off. He had followed the car for nearly half a mile!

That reminded me of an experience with one of those wasps many years ago, when we were getting started on that rented farm.

I wasn't concerned about a nest of yellow jackets that had taken up residence in the bank of the brook, out near the little plank bridge that I had crossed late every afternoon on my way after cows all summer.

This afternoon, two-year-old Terry was taking a later than normal nap, and I hurried out to get the cows in before she awoke. She couldn't walk far, or fast, with the burdensome hip-length brace she wore for her second year, and with my asthma, it was an ordeal for me to carry her, although I had to, nearly every day.

I was hurrying when I crossed the bridge, and didn't even see the hornet until he buzzed aggressively in my face, and nailed me right between the eyes. It hurt—oh, how it hurt!—but the pain was nothing beside the rage I felt at being attacked.

I went back to the house for a handful of matches, pumped a couple of quarts of gasoline into a can, and marched to the bridge. I scored a bulls-eye with the splash of gas into the nest, and followed it with a perfectly tossed match. It whoomph-ed into flame, and the hornets outside of the conflagration immediately launched an angry attack on the fire. I could hear the satisfying crackle of hornet kami-kazis, as I splashed brook water on my eyes, which were now swollen nearly shut, and then I stumbled off to bring in the cows.

DECISIONS, DECISIONS

I can't remember now just whose bright idea it was for us to take up bow hunting, but take it up we did. My brothers and I had fooled around with homemade bows when we were kids, but now my husband bought real bows, some blunt practice arrows, and some with razor-sharp hunting tips. And then we set out to learn how to use them.

My brother, Howard, was once again, helping us out with haying, and he took to it like the natural hunter he is. Merl and I were no slouches with rifles, so we soon caught the hang of it, too. We set up bales of hay in the little field across the road from the house, and we managed to get off a few practice shots nearly every time we came out of the house or barn. Satisfied with our progress as fall drew near, we obtained our hunting permits, and eagerly anticipated bow season.

Came the first day of the season, and my men folks had their hunting plan. They would approach Dutton's wooded brook from the northeast and the east. They wanted me to go farther west up the brook, then cross the field above it toward them. At the appointed time, I dutifully trudged up over the pasture hill to the brook, and slowly made my way up the little winding valley. About 300 feet along, there was an opening on the steep wooded south slope, where a spring seep and marshy ground kept the hemlock trees at bay. The semi-clearing led up to the neighbor's back field. I turned there, and silently, step by step, made my way up.

Moving so slowly and quietly, I didn't disturb any wildlife. Even the birds continued their twittering. And then I heard something else. I stopped, and tried to see what was coming along the slope. There was little vision through the thick hemlocks and underbrush. It took a while, but finally I saw it. At first, I thought it was a raccoon. It was the right size, but the odd undulating gait wasn't exactly coon-like. I waited, still as a stone.

The creature moved into the opening, and I realized that it was a fisher cat, although I had never seen one. It came across just above me, and I thought it wasn't going to notice me. I was wrong.

Suddenly aware that I was an unfamiliar object, the animal stopped abruptly, and eyed me warily. He came a step or two closer, sniffing, and peering. Then he sat up and squinted more closely. Not satisfied, he crept nearer, step by step, puzzled. Finally, right at my feet, he stopped and peered up at me, then sniffed my knee. I held stiff, waiting to see what he would do next. Finally convinced that I was something foreign, but that I was neither edible nor a threat, he turned and continued on his way, undulating like an otter out of sight into the underbrush on the other side of the clearing. Satisfied that I had just had an experience few people have, I went on up the hill.

I didn't see any deer that day, and went along home just before dusk. I knew where I would see deer, though, so my next trip to the brook valley was solo, about an hour before dark the next day I made my way up it. About half way to my destination I startled a doe. It bounded across the brook and hovered just inside the tree line. I moved on a few steps, and then realized what was going on. In my stealthy approach, I had walked between the doe and her fawn! I walked on, the fawn joined its mother, and I reached the bend where the brook disappeared into heavy woods to the northwest. I found a spot facing the small clearing where the deer came down out of the hardwoods late every afternoon, and congregated for a bit before they went on down to the river valley. I backed up to a small pine grove, and crouched there quietly, while I waited for the woods to come back to normal.

Ten minutes went by, fifteen. Still no birds singing, no squirrels scurrying. I couldn't figure it out. Other times, when I had gone up there just to watch the little drama, the woods would be noisy and cheerful within fifteen minutes of my arrival. I would wait until, just before dusk, it became suddenly silent, and a couple of doe would marvelously materialize without a sound. They would stand at the edge of the clearing, testing the wind for a time, then would move out and begin to graze. And soon the hillside would come alive with cracking twigs and running hooves, as the whole herd came bounding down to join them. There must have been nearly thirty of them at that time.

I would watch them graze and play, bucking and jumping like spring calves, then, once again, everything would become absolutely quiet. And then two bucks would step into the clearing, It amazed me: the females venture into the opening had proved safe, so now they could come out! They reminded me of the male hippies facing riot police at anti-war demonstrations some years before shouting, "Chicks up front!"

But this afternoon, no birds had resumed singing. I crouched there, watching for the first doe to appear, but clearly the woods were on alert. Finally, with darkness setting in, I stood up to leave--and that doe I had startled earlier snorted right at the back of my neck, and stamped! My own startled jump put her to flight, which was fortunate, because I would have felt no compunction about letting an arrow fly at her. She had stalked me, and had been silently standing there behind me for how long?

I made my way home, a bit humiliated.

I tried again a few days later, settling into a comfortable crouch against those same small pines. All the does had come out, but one came down onto the little flat where I was. I set about stalking her to get close enough for a sure shot. I could take a cautious step or two while she had her head down, grazing, then freeze in place while she raised her head and looked around, than repeat. We were about twenty feet apart when she realized that I was something she hadn't noticed before.

No dummy, she was immediately suspicious, and stepped mincingly toward me, peering intently. I didn't move a muscle, my bow held only halfway to shooting position. I watched her sniff, trying to identify what I was, with her getting more nervous by the moment. She stamped and snorted, and I managed not to flinch. She took a few tentative steps closer. Now I could get off a good quick shot right behind the shoulder as she turned.

And now I had a lot to consider.

If I shot her (and I didn't doubt that I could get in a fatal shot) she wouldn't die immediately, the best I could do. It would be one thing to shoot her with a rifle right between her eyes, and have her drop without pain, and quite another to let her run off with the arrow in her, and wait for her to bleed out before I tracked her. Also, I was nearly a mile from home, with some rugged up and down country to drag her through to take her back. And finally, I really don't like venison.

I do like to shoot.

I relaxed and lowered the bow.

"You'd better get out of here, or your momma's little fool is going to be in big trouble."

It is a wonder she didn't drop dead of a heart attack. She leaped high as she turned and disappeared like a shot.

I couldn't get that largest buck out of my mind, though. No one else knew about him and his buddy, so I once again made my way up to my waiting place the first day of regular deer season.

Once again, the does came out. Once again, they grazed and frolicked. And I waited. And waited. It was full dusk before the silence fell, and those two crafty creatures slipped out into the open. I couldn't be sure which ones they were. I was fairly sure they had come around on the edge of the flat next to me, and I tried to convince myself that it was still daylight enough for it to be legal to shoot one, but I couldn't see the antlers. I lay down on my stomach and tried to see him against the sky. No luck.

I stood and walked toward the herd, rifle tucked under my arm, climbing the little bank up to their flat. None of them noticed me and it was now dark enough that I couldn't make out individual animals. I was literally right in the middle of the bunch of them when one took fright and sounded the alarm.

The problem was that while the whole herd was thoroughly alarmed, they didn't know what they were alarmed about or where it was! I had a moment of alarm myself as they all milled in panic around me, and scattered with snorts and thundering hooves in all directions.

"Well," I muttered, "that wasn't too bright, was it?"

Not too many years later, Interstate 89 came through that valley just above the spot where the deer congregated every evening. Traversing their familiar ancestral route from the high hardwoods to the river valley, they were picked off one by one as they crossed that new obstruction.

I haven't been back there since.

PARTY LINE

Our number, on our rural Vermont eight party telephone lone, back in the 1930s through the 1950s, was seven-eight-ring-five…five short rings. When the operator rang our number, for a caller who was not on our line, the five rings were crisp and even. When one of our party-line neighbors rang, the result was usually much more hesitant and unprofessional. A Telephone Operator ring, which we identified readily, could be Long Distance, so it was imperative to answer it without delay, even if it meant getting bread dough all over the receiver. On long distance calls, you sometimes had to ask the neighbors on the line to hang up so you could hear the caller. Too many of them listening in on your call put such a strain on the batteries, the signal was very weak.

"Rubbering" on the party line was a time-honored tradition, and a major country recreation, although everyone who indulged in it would have suffered torture before she (or he) would ever admit to doing it. I remember my mother nearly having apoplexy one day, when she listened to a new bride calling her mother to ask how to make gravy. The mother told her to mix corn starch with water, and the girl didn't have any corn starch. The mother was completely stymied. Mom nearly popped a gusset to keep from blurting out that flour worked just as well. It required a bit of finesse to remove the receiver of the old wall telephone without making the least bit of sound, then to hold the palm of the hand over the mouthpiece to prevent any errant noise from your own household to enter it as you listened in on your neighbor's call. Any conversation you conducted on a party line needed to be on topics you wouldn't mind reading about in the weekly local newspaper.

Not everyone managed to escape detection, however. The genial gentleman who married my aunt in her later years was an inveterate rubberier, once he had retired. My aunt warned him that he would get caught. One day my mother was on the line when the old family clock in his living room chimed loud and clear. "And how are you today, Nelson?" my mother asked. He was red-faced and flustered; my aunt bent double with laughter.

My best friend and I devised a way to get rid of the elderly maiden sisters who haunted our every phone conversation. Gladys called me every morning to check on whether I would be wearing a skirt, dress or slacks to school, so she could dress accordingly.

"When I tell you what I'm going to wear tomorrow morning, you say 'okay' and then take the receiver away from your ear," I instructed her after school one day. Next morning I did, and she did, then I placed the earpiece against the mouthpiece. It emitted the loudest, most unearthly screech imaginable. We were well pleased with ourselves and the line was clear for us for quite a while.

The party line worked well for summoning help in an emergency. The caller simply turned the crank vigorously for several seconds, until all the neighbors reached their phones. The crisis (whether chimney fire, accident, or lost child) and the location could then be described one time for everyone, and help was on the way immediately.

My future husband and I had returned from a date late one August Saturday night in 1950, and were sitting in the dooryard making plans for a trip to Ausable Chasm in New York State for the next day, when we heard that prolonged ring. We looked around the horizon for evidence of fire and saw a glow to the east over Kent's Ledge.

"That's my barn!" he exclaimed, and ran to start the truck.

It was a huge glow by the time we drove the five miles to his dairy farm. The house was saved and fortunately most of the cows were out in the night pasture, but he lost his cow dog, who he'd left hitched in the barn, the whole summer's store of hay, and a lot of equipment.

That same ring summoned help when my brother, then six years-old, went missing one evening. The woods around our little farm were filled with dozens of willing searchers in half an hour. All ended happily when he was finally discovered sound asleep under some quilts in the attic over the woodshed, where he'd gone when his brother and I had promised he would be in big trouble with our parents over some major mischief he had done. We were astonished (and somewhat disappointed) that all he got were hugs and kisses instead of the spanking he richly deserved!

It was fun trying to guess which neighbor was calling by the expertise (or lack of expertise) in ringing our number. We got fairly expert at guessing. One frequent caller was a neighboring farmer. He and his wife were pals of my folks, although I sometimes wondered how my parents could enjoy so much of their company. He wasn't the sharpest knife in the drawer and my dad was very witty and funny. The phone rang one afternoon when I was sitting at the kitchen table with Mom and Dad. Very clumsy ring-ring-ring-ring…. Dad knew it was his friend, and stood halfway up, then froze, waiting for the next and final ring.

"Well, what's the matter with him?" he exclaimed.

"He's trying to remember what comes after four," I said.

MISCALCULATION

That truck tire incident always reminds me of a certain episode on the old TV sitcom, *WKRP in Cincinnatti*. The station manager had been arrested for bombing a shopping center with live turkeys as a Thanksgiving day promotion. The station manager, played by Gordon Jump, said earnestly, "As God is my witness, I thought turkeys could fly!"

Our Dad had brought home a used truck tire, intending to hitch it to a maple limb for a swing. Before he bought the rope, we were putting the tire to good use.

Harold and I started with our younger brother, Howard. We had him sit in the center, tucking in his hands and feet, as we held it upright, and then we rolled him carefully around the yard. Harold and I took turns rolling each other. It was almost as good as a ride at Tunbridge Fair, whirling about head over heels.

Then Cousin Ira came along, and he wanted a ride. We settled him in and rolled him up across the dooryard toward the garage. Back across the dooryard we came, and onto the lawn. The lawn lay level in front of the house, then sloped down toward the road. At the edge of the lawn, the bank dropped off about four feet to the gravel roadway. We whisked

Ira across to the slope, and gave an extra push.

"Hang on!" we yelled.

The tire rolled down to the edge, landed right in the middle of the road, then in one magnificent bound, completely cleared the wall and wire fence on the far side! On and on he went, bouncing and spinning down across Dewey's pasture, to finally fetch up far below in a clump of young pine trees, unhurt, but understandably upset.

We were long gone before he trudged his way back up to the dooryard, and we gave him plenty of room until he cooled off.

As God is my witness, I thought the stonewall would stop that tire.

CRIME AND PUNISHMENT

The Barney Fife character on the old TV show Mayberry, USA had to have been modeled on the old school patrolman of my youth. Those students designated for this singular honor were issued white patrolmen's cross shoulder belts, badges, and in too many cases, an inflated sense of their own power and authority.

Hard as it may now be to believe, when I was young, I seldom tested or defied authority. The world ran on rules, and I was content with that, no matter what my opinion of some of them might be. I put with bossy patrolman, although I felt perfectly capable of crossing a street without their assistance by the time I went to high school in South Royalton. I could be pushed only so far, however.

That day there was a January thaw. It had snowed overnight, and the streets and sidewalks were bordered by slushy snow. During the noon hour, I decided to scoot up to the village business block to the stationery store to pick up some supplies. A School Patrolman stood at the intersection of the main block, and I obediently followed his instructions in crossing the side street. A group of high school boys were lounging against the building on the other side. I went into the store, completed my business, and hurried out to return to school.

As I neared the crossing, I could see that boys were up to no good. They were in high spirits, and, as I stepped into the street, they began to pelt me with snowballs. I ran to the other side to get out of their range.

"You can't run across the street!" Barney Fife yelled at me.

"Make them stop throwing snowballs, and I'll walk!"

"You go back across the street and walk back!" he ordered.

"If you want to exercise your authority, make them stop, you coward!"

"I told you to go back across the street and walk back!"

I had a few more choice words for him, that I judiciously choked down unsaid. I walked back across, warding off the missiles, scooped up a good handful of snow, turned around and came back to the patrolman. I smacked the wad of snow into his face and ground it around a turn or two.

"How do you like it, you darned sissy!"

The high school principal motioned me out of class that afternoon. The patrolman had tattled.

I explained what happened in vivid detail, and got an instant illustration of the old axiom that "the lawyer who represents himself, has a fool for a client." The man was unmoved, although I detected much amusement behind his stern demeanor.

I can't have my patrolmen getting killed or maimed." he said.

My sentence was to wait for fifteen minutes after school every day until the patrol went off duty. I left the office in a purple fury at the injustice, and with some very unworthy thoughts swirling in my head.

I waited after the last bell for fifteen minutes for about

three weeks, and the principal still hadn't let me off the hook. I went into his office one day and asked how long I had to keep that up.

"Are you still doing that?" he asked.

EVERY DOG HAS ITS DAY

It was one of those idyllic balmy spring days that are the reason Vermonters endure months of winter and mud season. I was planting the last of the garden, while Terry "helped" me and Diane cooed in her baby buggy. Bees hummed in the Duchess Apple tree at the end of the garden, and a lovely fragrance from the orchard higher on the hill wafted down.

My lovely morning was shattered by the arrival of an irate neighbor. I came down out of the garden as he stormed around his pickup.

"Don't you know enough to fix fence before you turn your cattle out?" he shouted. "I'm getting sick and tired of being yelled at by people when it's not even my young stock!"

He continued to vent loudly along the same lines, while I looked him calmly in the eye and said nothing. Terry crept down, and peeped at him from behind my leg.

I was interested in seeing him so furious. He was normally a quiet, genial little man, while his wife was usually the one blowing a gasket at or about someone.

"You've got seven Jersey heifers and a Holstein bull running loose on Broad Brook Road! They've been tearing up lawns and gardens all the way to East Barnard! That bull has a rope around his neck that is too tight, and you're going to find yourself in trouble with the law if you don't do something about it!"

It was the first opportunity I'd had to get a word in.

"And what else does your wife say?"

He gasped in indignation, and I quietly cut him off at the knees.

"Number one, we don't have a bull. Number two, we don't own a Holstein. And number three, we haven't turned any cattle out yet. They're all in the barn."

It was really a shame to squash the only heroic effort I'd ever known him to undertake. But my, my, my, it felt good!

The truant cattle belonged to a cattle dealer over on Broad Brook, we learned later.

We took extra time on line fences when we repaired them that year.

SNOWMOBILE RESCUE

It was in the early days of the snowmobile in Vermont when you could still drive wherever you wanted, and it opened up the possibility that you could go a lot farther by snowmobile in a relatively short time than you could safely struggle back if your machine broke down. People were enthusiastically ranging far and wide.

My husband was the town's Civil Defense chairman at that time, and it occurred to him that it would be better to have a snowmobile rescue plan in place than to wait until the need arose. Since most of the volunteer firemen and rescue people were also avid snowmobilers, they were the natural group to make up the squad. Merl started by having a town highway map blown up to a four-by-four wall hanging, then drew a grid of the whole town on it, and numbered the blocks. Two man teams would be assigned certain blocks, would search them, and then report back to receive new assignments.

They tested the system one cold sunny Saturday. Merl went up with Dr. Ron Gadway in his plane, and dropped some inflated balloons (not helium filled.) The rescue squad was called out. Each team of two had received their grid assignments, all in the east part of the town, and set out. Two wise guys thought they could get a leg up on the rest of them, so they stopped in to talk with a farmer

"Did you see any balloons come down?" they asked.

"Balloons?" the farmer echoed. They went along on their search, and the farmer glanced up again at the balloon hanging in the tree in his front yard and grinned.

It was a tired, rather disgruntled crew who gathered in the firehouse later to dissect their experience. Some were of the opinion that it would be better to search on snowshoes in untracked woodland than try to break through on snowmobiles.

The first real alert came early one morning. Two teenagers had left on snowmobiles the evening before and hadn't returned home. Once again the squad assembled. And just as they were setting out came a phone call. One of the teenagers had finally had the presence of mind to call his parents to tell them where they were. They had stopped at the camp of friends in the next town, and had played poker all night.

The rescue crew decided that what they needed was a real person to be stranded somewhere in town, so they could test their preparedness. I volunteered to be the lost victim. It would be a nighttime search because the volunteers had jobs in the daytime. The men had a fit when they heard that I would be going alone. I finally agreed to take along my friend.

On the day of the "search" a few of us went up to the area where I would be lost and broke out a lot of aimless trails. The men had also I insisted that someone should know exactly where I would be. Okay. My father was also thoroughly familiar with the area and I told him where I intended to wait.

The spot I had chosen was in the woods there I had spent my childhood and I knew it well. It was a rugged wooded rectangle with ledges, valleys and hills; roughly two miles wide at each end, and more than three miles long. At four o'clock, my friend and I headed our snowmobiles up an old wood road where we had come down earlier in the day. I was in the lead (and we were almost to our destination) when I ran a front ski over a spruce branch that was frozen in the track. The spruce was an ancient one that sat about four feet above the road. Its big lower branch had been bowed clear down to the road by a heavy snowfall and frozen in. As I crossed it, the end broke and snapped, catching me in the forehead and sweeping me to the back of the machine. Only the backrest kept me from being brushed right off. I stopped, ears ringing, lights flashing in my head. I had had a wool headband on; it was gone. I saw it and staggered over to retrieve it. I felt my face, and realized that only the headband had kept me from having the skin split to the bone.

My friend came up on her snowmobile and I got back on my machine. We continued to where we drove them off the road and shut them off. I took the "survival kit" that I always carried out of the "trunk," and led the way up over the small open knoll above the wood road. Just over the top was a slanting ledge that was about five feet high. We walked down around that and set up camp against it. There were two trees below it about ten feet apart, so I tied clothesline across at the back, and another across from two boughs at the front, then laid my ten-by-twenty foot plastic drop cloth on the ground, and pulled it up over the back line and out across the front, making a dry place to sit, with a good windbreak from the north.

It was nearly dark, and my friend had broken through the snow crust and twisted her knee painfully, so I went into the nearby dense stand of young spruce and tugged out some dead trees which were about fifteen feet tall. (My head felt like a drum corps was practicing in it.) That done, I took a few curls of outer bark from a fallen white birch nearby, broke some little dead twigs from the spruce, and started a small fire in front of our lean-to, then added larger sticks. With a good flame going, I dragged up a couple of the trees, pulled one across the fire a couple of feet, and crisscrossed another one in the same way over it. My friend was puzzled.

"No point in wasting energy in chopping wood when it will burn through and do it for me," I said. When the pieces burned through, I placed them in the fire, drew the trees up and crossed them again. Delightfully simple. I set my little pot on with snow in it to melt. With the water hot, we each had a cup of hot chocolate, and roasted hotdogs over the coals.

My husband wanted a way to keep in touch with us through the evening, so we each had a walkie-talkie which we activated each half hour. (I didn't say anything about our injuries.) It was on a popular CB band, so we could hear our "rescuers" talking to each other. At the start of the evening, they were in high spirits, thinking they would come on us quickly, bring in the rescue gear, sled us out, and go back to the firehouse to rehash their fun. As the hours wore on, however, and no one had found any trace of us, the chatter became worried. None of them could imagine two women staying that long in the woods without something being very wrong.

It was nearly midnight when one team finally topped our knoll and looked down at us cheerfully stoking our fire and drinking cocoa. They seemed very annoyed that we weren't at death's door.

Without another word, they set off down the trail we had come up. Shortly thereafter I got a call from my husband.

"The guys say it's so late that they are going to skip the rescue exercise," he said. "You can come along down."

"Our machines are over the bank, and we don't feel good, so, if you're not coming up after us, we'll just stay here until morning." I said.

"I'll be right up," he said. A couple of the other men came with him, and pulled the sleds into the road. The lights had quit working on mine. We took my friend home, and joined a couple of the men at the firehouse. Merl was discussing the exercise with them when he happened to turn to look at me.

"What happened to you?!" he exclaimed.

"A branch snapped and hit me in the forehead," I said. Apparently my face was very white and one of my pupils was much larger than the other.

"We'd better get you to a doctor!"

"No, I've lived with it this long, I'll wait until morning."

And I did.

ME AND THE NORTHERN STRATEGIC AIR COMMAND

People have accused me of being a bit unbalanced, even paranoid, if you will, on the subject of telephone cables. I have given the matter serious thought, and have decided that, considering the history of my experiences with telephone cables, I can live with that. And, if anyone wants my company, they'll just have to live with it. I have been severely traumatized in the past, and I know, as long as those galvanized things hang out there in front of my house, looping their slinky lengths from pole to pole, that it may happen again.

One incident began, as have so many others in my life, innocently enough. A good friend had been very ill, and was still nervous about being alone, so I had been going over each night to stay with her while she recuperated. This particular evening, my family was all in bed, it was quite late, and heavy wet snow was still accumulating. We had a good four-wheel-drive vehicle, so I wasn't concerned about the hills or the miles I would be driving, but I found, as the road climbed, and as the snow depth increased, more and more trees were bent double, and hung over in the road.

In the middle of the steepest, longest hill, I came upon a large yellow birch that had broken under the load, and its top nearly covered the highway. The only thing that held it from crashing right across the road was a fat telephone cable that was now drawn as taut as the A-string on a fiddle.

My friend was up, waiting for me when I arrived, and, before we started our nightly gabfest, I looked up the number for the telephone emergency repair service, and gave them a call. A female voice answered.

"Are you a residence or business number?" asked the voice.

I told her that my call didn't concern a specific phone, but a whole phone line.

That didn't compute.

"Are you a business or residential telephone?"

Again, I tried to explain my reason for calling. She was losing patience with me.

"What number are you reporting?" she wanted to know.

I wasn't reporting a number, I said, I wanted to report a tree down on a main telephone line.

"We don't do trees."

"Look," I explained patiently, "this tree is on a telephone cable that is stretched almost to the breaking point. It would save a lot of expense and a lot of inconvenience to a lot of people if it is dealt with now instead of after the cable breaks."

"Well, we don't take down trees. Maybe if you call your local Parks Department…."

The day that Sharon, Vermont, has a Parks Department is probably the day cows learn to use computers, but that was beside the point.

"Listen closely," I told her, in the tones I usually reserve for balky teenagers and other particularly dense, obstinate life forms, "there is a large tree hanging on a New England Telephone cable in the middle of Howe Hill, in the town of Sharon, Vermont, and it is very likely to snap said cable before morning. Now, maybe you have no interest in that fact, but I can assure you that there are other people in your company, and a myriad of captive rate-payers, and, for all I know, the whole of the Northeast Strategic Air Command who do take an intense interest in it! Now put me through to your supervisor, you ignorant twit!"

I was shouting at a dial tone.

I re-dialed the number in a scarlet fury. It was a blessing for all of us that the person who fielded that second call had both hemispheres of her brain intact. We contracted our business amicably, and three hours later, I could finally fall asleep.

There is a reason why the prospect of all those little multicolored wire ends hanging out of a ruptured cable filled me with such a sense of urgency. It wasn't the first time I had witnessed it.

The first time was one Labor Day weekend, when Merl and I became aware that a crew of telephone linemen was working around the clock on the cable that ran along the road down below the railroad track on the farm we rented during our first years of married life. For three days and nights they were there, with someone working diligently on the cable at all times, swaying in a seat suspended between the two poles.

"Boy, that's costing some overtime," we told each other.

I had forgotten all about it, when I drove happily home from a grocery shopping trip one afternoon, a few days later.

There was a state police cruiser parked in the yard, and my husband was talking with the officer beside it. I bolted out of the pickup to see what was wrong.

"He says someone shot down through the telephone cable the other day," Merl said.

I thought it over.

"There's no way anyone could shoot down through it," I said. "No one could get high enough above it to do that."

"That's what I said," Merl continued. "He wanted to know if we knew of anyone who had been shooting around here last Friday. I told him you had."

I bowed to him silently, vowing to thank him properly when I got him alone.

"Were you shooting at 8:01 a.m. last Friday?" the officer asked me.

I had to consider that for a while. If anyone had asked me if I bombed Pearl Harbor on December 7, 1941, I'd have to stop and think back to just what I had been doing that day before I could deny it.

"Yes," I said, finally, remembering. "The red squirrels are raising hob with my chicken grain, and I was thinning them out a little. But I wasn't shooting toward the telephone line. I was shooting up into those trees there. I got all but one of them, and he hasn't chewed a grain bag since."

"Could I see the gun?" he asked.

"Sure."

I went inside and came out with the little pump .22 I used for rodent control. He jacked and checked the empty chamber, then examined it from end to end, and handed it back to me.

"Now, just what was it you were doing with it?"

I explained that the squirrels had scurried out of the henhouse when I went in that morning, and the cow dog had chased them up those trees below the railroad track, but high above the telephone lines. When I finished tending the hens, I went into the house, got the rifle, loaded up, and started to pick them off, to the great delight of Pat, our collie shepherd, who didn't know she wasn't hired as a hunting dog.

I had gotten four with my first four shots, but the fifth squirrel didn't present a clear shot. I wasted two shells on him, and then went into the milk house where Merl was finishing up.

"Come see what you can do," I challenged him, perturbed that I was having such an off day. He didn't have any better luck, and we gave it up and went in to breakfast.

"The only think I can think of," Merl said, "is that one of her shots must have ricocheted down through the cable."

I made more mental notes of the thanks that I owed him.

But this wasn't the situation the trooper had been expecting to encounter. Nor had the telephone company. They had been experiencing a rash of malicious shooting-up of their lines and equipment, and they intended to deal severely with the vandal who had done this costly deed. I think the trooper was beginning to feel sorry for me—whether for the predicament I was in, or for having such a disloyal tattletale for a husband, I could only guess.

"I can't promise you anything," the officer told me, "but I'll explain what happened, and maybe they'll be willing to take into account that it was an accident."

We were still engaged in a friendly conservation when the five o'clock passenger train went through. The engineer froze in mid-wave and completely forgot his customary beep-beep in greeting. He and the fireman were both hanging out the window, looking back, as they rounded the curve above our place, bug-eyed at the sight of the state trooper with his back to his cruiser, while I stood facing him with a rifle in my hands.

A couple of days later, I had done a number of errands in White River Junction, and was on my way home, when I came upon a state police roadblock. It was a routine vehicle inspection check, but I had a burnt out headlight. I went through the check routine, then handed the officer my own shopping list along with the requested license and registration.

"See? Right there!" I said. "'Buy headlight!'"

I picked up the new lamp from the seat beside me, and

shook it in his face. He grinned and made out the ticket. It wasn't a summons, but receiving it meant that, instead of installing the new light ourselves, we'd have to hire an official inspection shop to do it, so they could certify to the state that we had taken care of the infraction within forty-eight hours.

At home, I had just changed my clothes, when there was a knock on the door. It was the officer who had investigated the shooting.

"It's a conspiracy," I said. "You guys have been talking to each other, haven't you? "How did you know I was going to White River today?"

He laughed.

"Got caught in the road check, huh?" he said. Then he became more serious.

"How many squirrels did you say you got that morning?"

"Four."

"Oh! Well, I told 'em five. They were impressed. And they aren't going to press charges!"

I came very close to hugging a cop on duty. I thanked him profusely.

He then told me why this case was viewed with such gravity. Back then, the Strategic Air Command communications' system used the Bell systems, with the specific lines being utilized a highly classified secret, and their routes changed periodically to ensure their security. As my luck would have it, that Friday morning, sensitive defense communiqués could have been flashing through that dull cable when my squirrel hunting put an end to them. He said there was a special gas in the line, and its release, when the line was severed, triggered the registering of the exact time of the mishap.

A few years later, my brother, Howard, was working for us

during haying, and we were all quite taken with archery. We didn't have much time for practice, but Merl and Howard would usually try to get in a few shots after lunch, while I finished up in the kitchen.

We had a target set up on the lawn across the road against a backdrop of hay bales, and they began to lob their first shot each day long distance, from the porch.

This day, they listened to be sure no cars were coming, both drew, and aiming high to allow for the distance, they let drive. There was the resounding "twang," and one of the arrows twirled down from a dead-on encounter with my old friend, the telephone cable. An inspection didn't reveal any overt damage from the blunt practice arrow, but Merl decided he'd better report it to the phone company.

"Don't you dare say I had anything to do with this!" I warned him.

The telephone personnel were not happy, but they later confirmed that no damage had been done. However, it reminded me once again of the final word on that earlier episode with the squirrels.

It was several nights after the trooper had returned to tell me that no charges would be brought, that Merl suddenly sat straight up in bed. "Do you remember when you asked me to come out and try to get that last squirrel that day?"

"Yes."

Do you recall that last shot I made—there was a funny "twang' when it hit the oak tree, and I remember thinking it was an odd noise.

"I'm the one who put the bullet through the telephone cable!"

THE LADY OF THE HOUSE

As one who is such an easy mark for magazine or book offers or seed and garden stock, it is difficult to explain how, over the years, I have sent so many salesmen weeping to their therapists. Perhaps some of it has just been a matter of unfortunate timing. That surely explains the incident with that new salesman one afternoon.

There's an old saw among writers that says writing is one percent inspiration and ninety-nine percent perspiration. I'd say that's about right…the seat of the pants applied to the seat of the chair in front of the computer until something reasonably literate and acceptable comes up.

But some days it's not like that at all. Once in a while an idea strikes and all you have to do is sit and write it down as it develops, and that makes up for all the times you've had to labor and grind out each syllable.

I was having one of those rare joyous days and was well into a story, which was pleasing me more and more as I typed each paragraph…when the doorbell rang.

Now, I have been known to ignore as many as six rings of the phone under certain circumstances, but I find it very difficult to be equally strong-minded about a doorbell ring. I let it ring twice, hoping the caller would give up then on the third ring, with a sigh of resignation, I went out to answer it.

It was the man with the brushes. Or rather, it was a new man with the brushes, fresh from his sales training seminar. Now I was a regular customer of the former route man, but this was just not the day when I wished to consider cleaning products.

He started his pitch. Still trying to hold on to my train of thought, I interrupted to tell him that I was very busy, but would be glad to talk with him another time.

"Is your oven dirty?" he demanded.

Goodbye, story.

I gave him my full and undivided attention as he waved a spray can in my face.

"My oven is always dirty," I assured him. He could smell victory. Taking a roll of paper towels from his case, he swept into the kitchen. Opening the oven door, he doused it liberally with his wonder spray. I watched, hands on my hips. He closed the oven door and expounded on the substance's virtues as he waited for it to do its work.

Finally came the moment of truth.

He wadded up a liberal handful of towel, opened the oven door, and made a dramatic swipe at the charred puddle in the bottom of the oven.

Nothing happened.

He scrubbed frantically at it.

Still nothing.

"This isn't grease!"

"No, it's apple pie juice."

"But you said your oven was greasy!"

"No, you asked if my oven were dirty, and I said it's always dirty. You didn't ask me about grease."

He glared at me and at the offending oven. I rinsed out a dishcloth, and handed it to him.

"Please wipe up your spray," I told him nicely, "I have to get back to work."

I'm not the only meanie in my family, however, and I've never been able to bring myself up to my husband's level. That poor brush man's trauma didn't begin to equal that of the insurance salesman who approached Merl one day.

Now common sense alone, to say nothing of sales training sessions, should tell you that if you interrupt, on a clear hot summer day, a farmer who is welding a piece of hay equipment in his yard, you won't have a very receptive prospect. This fellow was either very obtuse, or had a latent death wish.

It took three tries for him to get Merl's attention. Merl was wearing a welding helmet, the machine was humming, the rod was buzzing and spitting as it made contact. He was concentrating on his task, and had no idea that anyone was near him.

Two cheery "good mornings" hadn't elicited response, so the salesman tapped Merl on the shoulder. Merl jumped and flipped up his face mask.

"Good morning, sir! May I have just a minute of your time?"

"Not today," snapped Merl, fairly graciously, I thought considering circumstances.

"All I need is one minute," begged the man.

Merl nodded grimly, still squatting beside his work, and the salesman launched eagerly into his pitch. He had barely warmed to the lead-in when Merl looked at his watch.

"Your minute is up," he said, flipping down the face mask. The welding arc glowed its unbearably bright phosphorescent brilliance and sizzled and hissed like a bad temper.

The salesman stood looking helplessly at Merl's back, then returned forlornly to his car.

Not all of the sales pitches drive into our yard, however.

It was just a few weeks after Tunbridge Fair when I received the impressive-looking letter.

"Congratulations," it read. I was the ducky-lucky second place winner of a super sewing machine, a marvel of this technological age, which would zig, zag, change its own bobbin, and do everything but unstick a balky zipper.

All I had to do was come down to Laconia, New Hampshire, to the salesroom to pick up that wondrous sewing machine head...and pick out a cabinet for it for the nominal sum of $129.95. I knew when they told me I had only won second place there was going to be a hitch.

What I wanted to know, though, was who had entered my name in their drawing? They had sent my "stub' back and the printed name and address were nothing I had filled out, absent-mindedly or otherwise. I mentioned the letter at the supper table, and Terry and Diane burst into delighted laughter.

"Second place! We thought maybe if we wrote your name, it would bring you better luck!"

"Thanks for thinking of me," I said sourly.

A few days later, an identical announcement arrived--some people have no faith in Uncle Sam's mail service--and I placed it in File 13.

The next week brought a personal letter. I should really hurry down to pick up my winnings while there was a wide selection of cabinets. (Don't tell me there was more than one second place winner!) I wadded it up and did a bank shot off the wall into the wastebasket.

A few days later a plaintive little note arrived. They were perplexed, and hurt too, I gathered, that I hadn't come down to pick up my prize. And it ended with a dark warning. If I didn't show within ten days, they would have to award my super-duper sewing machine to a runner-up.

That did it. Award my prize to someone else? Immediately, I dashed off a letter to them.

…You can't know how thrilled I was to be a winner in your drawing. I have never won anything like that in my life! However, I have a perfectly good sewing machine cabinet, to which I am very much attached, so if you would let me know when it would be convenient for you, I'll come down and pick up just the head I won. I'll be waiting to hear from you.

That was several years ago, and I'm still waiting. But, as you may have noticed, I'm not holding my breath.

FENCES…AND NEIGHBORS

Foggy August mornings sometimes held surprises on our farm on the White River in east central Vermont. I learned that a telephone call at 7:00 a.m. seldom bodes any good.

I was putting breakfast on when it rang one gloomy morn. The supervisor of the construction crew on Interstate 89 was on the line.

"Are you missing a horse?"

I looked in the general direction of the horse pasture. The fog was so dense I couldn't see across the lawn.

"How in the world would I know?"

"Well, we have one up above Royalton. We caught him and have him hitched. If I come down and get you, will you take a look?"

"Sure." I went to put on some sneakers.

Living in a narrow river valley, with a railroad track running down through it, makes a perfect trailway for any animal on the loose there. The unfinished interstate highway made an even nicer one. Usually heifers, tasting freedom, landed in village neighbors' yards. Since most town people are not agriculturally oriented, we (and another farm neighbor or two) had strained urban/rural relations for a time after the Vermont Supreme Court in its infinite wisdom ruled that land owners who didn't own livestock didn't have to maintain line fences. It sometimes took a while for farmers to make neglected neighbors' fences "horse high, bull strong, and hog tight" - the former criteria for what made good neighbors, and sensible law.

The problems on our place began in earnest when the interstate was being surveyed. The survey crews were extremely casual about closing gates, and we had irate village neighbors calling again and again. Merl had finally had enough. He called the state department in charge of the interstate construction. He explained, quite calmly, I thought, about the last matter of open gate/loose heifers, and told them they had to do something about it.

There was nothing they could do, he was informed. His calmness evaporated.

"Well, there's darn well something I can do about it!" he shouted. "Those (bleep bleeps) are down on my land right now. There's a big elm tree right by the gate they went through to get there. I'm taking my chainsaw up right now, and they'll be right there for a chat when they get through!"

"You can't do that!"

"Just watch me."

A carload of suits from Montpelier was in our dooryard in exactly one hour.

It came to a head the day the fence-building crew for the interstate arrived. Good hay day. Full day of work ahead. Blasted phone call.

"Your cows are in the village!"

Our cows were right where they belonged, but a frisky contingent of two-year-old heifers sure weren't. We rounded them up, drove them down the railroad track to the barnyard, and penned them up. After chores that night, we drove up around on the Oxbow Road to the west of our property to see how they got out.

The huge bulldozers were there, parked neatly for the night. A great swath of what had been our beautiful pine grove was down, and so was the fence. We drove down beside the devastation until we found the night watchman. Merl got out and went over to him.

"I know you had nothing to do with the fact that this morning this construction company turned thirty head of our heifers loose on the village, and to run on the highway and railroad track, but I have a message for the people who do have some responsibility for what goes on at this site. The agreement with the state was that the new fence would be constructed before the old one was removed. They overlooked that. I'm putting my heifers back in this pasture tomorrow morning, and if just one of them gets out because of this missing fence, those machines will never run again. I may spend the rest of my life in jail, but this is one bunch of outlaws who won't get away scot-free!"

The heifers didn't get out again.

Scarier than 7:00 a.m. calls, though, were the middle of the night alarms. One occurred on a sub-zero night at 1:00 a.m.

"This is the Central Vermont Railway. Our engineer on the midnight freight thinks he hit one of your horses."

"One" of our horses. We had sold 25 head the previous autumn when we closed our children's farm camp, keeping only our two older daughters' ponies. Where was the other one? We pulled on our clothes and went across the road to the crossing by the horse barn. Sure enough, there was the paint, nearly buried by the deep snow in the ditch on the other side of the track. No sign of the bay pony, though. They were kept in the field across the track, and the gate was securely closed. They would have had to get through the railroad fence to get on the track. We set out to look for Tony.

It was bitterly cold, but a beautiful night. We drove slowly up toward the village, looking across at the field, but no sign of him. However, there were tracks leading across our small field north of our next door neighbor's place. They were headed toward the track. I drove up to the village and let Merl off to walk south down the railroad track. I again drove down our home street, looking for any sign.

And then I saw a glimpse of movement in the north corner of the field across the track. I looked again, carefully, but didn't see it again. Nothing to do but get out and wade through the hip-deep snow across the small field, to cross the railroad track. Puffing asthmatically, I finally attained the height of the track.

There were both ponies, right where they belonged, ears up, looking at me! I struggled down into the snow-filled gully and up to the fence. The pretty little paint, Sundance, was there all right. I stroked his nose. And alive! I knew for sure. He bit me.

I went back to the track and headed north to meet Merl. He could hardly believe it, either. Now the problem was, whose horses had been making all the tracks? We made our way back to the car and again crept toward the village. Then we saw them coming off the track behind one the houses.

Merl leaped out and drove them back and up the track, while I went up to the village and around to the home of the retired gentleman, a local philanthropist, who now enjoyed his hobby of sheep and horses. Merl closed the barn door behind them just as the five o'clock passenger train roared through. We went home to do chores.

The man showed up in our barn that morning. He was sorrowful because the paint that was killed was the first horse he had bought years ago for his only daughter, but he was very grateful that we had caught the others in time. He held out a twenty-dollar bill to Merl.

"I won't take your money, John. I remember the dump trucks and the help you furnished when my barn burned. I really appreciated that."

He left with tears running down his cheeks.

A neighbor stopped to chat with Merl a few days later. He was feeling bad that John had lost his horse. They had been tramping around for more than a week, and had pawed up his and his neighbors' lawns.

"You knew they were getting out?"

"Yes, we thought they were yours."

So back to that foggy morning. I rode the three miles with the supervisor up to where they had the colt hitched. It belonged to that same neighbor. I told Bud where he belonged.

"Wouldn't you like to lead him home?" he asked hopefully.

"Nope," I said." I really wouldn't."

BLACKIE

"Only you could have a dog get hit by an airplane!" my friend told me.

I say it could have happened to anyone.

Blackie was a (mostly) border collie we kept from a litter of old Pat's puppies, in the mild hope of turning him into a first rate cow dog, too. From the beginning, Blackie had other ideas, and neither Merl nor I had time that summer to disabuse him of his notions, or to give him the constant attention required to make a working dog of him. Blackie became our daughters' mutt and companion.

From puppyhood, he loved to ride. In the back of the truck with the girls, his tail fanning happily, grinning open-mouthed into the wind, or on the front seat beside Merl, sitting erect and smug as a reigning monarch surveying his realm, Blackie was in his element. It took some rather firm discipline to convince him that there was no way that he could ride on the farm tractors, and to discourage him from bouncing perilously about the moving vehicles, begging for a ride.

When we bought an old snowmobile for Terry and Diane, Blackie immediately fell in love with it. As soon as one of them started it up, he pounced crossways onto the rear of the seat, and there he would cling, delirious with joy, as the machine sped around the fields.

But Blackie's single mindedness in attaining what he wanted sometimes got him into trouble. For several years after he was grown we had no problem with him leaving the dooryard, unless he was accompanying us on farm work. Then our young neighbors acquired a German shepherd puppy. It didn't take long to prove my father's adage:

You have to know more than the dog to train one.

The puppy became a neighborhood nuisance as soon as it was old enough to roam. It didn't take much encouragement for Blackie to join him. We put a stop to Blackie's rambling with a stout chain and shooed the other dog home every time he showed up. Later we relented on Blackie's confinement and let him off the chain during the day, as he appeared to have no inclination to run off.

This happy state of affairs was interrupted by a phone call one afternoon. The excited voice on the line belonged to an elderly neighbor who lived down beyond the shepherd's owners.

"Your dog is killing a deer down in the field!" she cried.

Sure enough, a quarter of a mile away, I could see a commotion of black, tan, and tawny bodies. I yelled at Blackie and to my utter surprise, he stopped and raised his head.

"You get yourself home this minute!" I shouted.

He set out obediently for home, then paused to look back at the shepherd and the deer.

"Don't even think it!" I yelled, and he continued the long way up to the dooryard, greeting me happily with wagging tail.

Heartsick, and angry again that the untrained German shepherd had contributed to Blackie's delinquency, I hooked him to the chain and went in to call the young neighbors. They weren't home.

It wasn't long before I saw the game warden's car go down through, turn off and head out to the deer. The shepherd was still there, but there was no shot, and I saw the dog trotting home shortly thereafter. Soon the car pulled into our yard. The warden scrutinized Blackie as he came up to the porch.

"Has your black dog there been loose today?" he asked politely.

I sighed, reluctant.

"Yes," I said. "It makes me so angry. For six years he never ran off until that cussed German shepherd started coming around, and he has never bothered deer feeding in the fields, but he was down there today, so if you have to take him, I guess you have to."

The warden began to grin. I glared at him, indignant at such a callous response.

"Do you know that you are the first dog owner who has ever admitted to me that your dog was loose?"

"Well, he was. I can't lie about it."

"He wasn't chasing a deer," he said. "That deer was already dead. It had been shot and it's stiff. They were just tossing it around and playing with it."

Blackie was summarily sentenced to the tether, except when we let him loose to accompany us on fieldwork, chores, or for a ride. He accepted it without much fuss. His delinquent companion continued to roam and soon began to chase cars that came infrequently by his house. That apparently didn't furnish enough excitement, so next he challenged the trains that also ran in front of his house. That game came abruptly to an end when he finally succeeded in biting a freight car wheel. A friend of the young neighbor woman called Merl.

"She saw her dog's body when she drove out this morning,

and she doesn't know what to do. Would you be willing to bury it?"

"I'd be happy to," Merl said, sincerely. And he was.

With no more loose companion to lure him into mischief, we tentatively let Blackie free more and more often. He was his old slaphappy, scatterbrained self.

Then late one afternoon, as I was working at the stove, and my daughters were doing homework at the kitchen table, I heard a racket on the porch. I hurried to the door, and Blackie barreled in, nearly knocking me off my feet. His face was bloody, and he was emitting the loudest, shrillest, most frightening piercing yelps I had ever heard. He raced through the kitchen, around the living room, back around the kitchen and the entry room, and into the kitchen.

Terry and Diane had grabbed little Lisa and leaped onto the kitchen counter and they were crying in shock and fright. I sidestepped him each time he blindly bore down on me, my ears hurting with his yells.

"Blackie!" I shouted, but he was completely out of his mind. I ran to the door as he made his next circle of the living room, and opened it as he came at me again. He raced out and straight into the hay barn. I hurried after him and pulled down the overhead door.

I went back to see to the girls, and not long after, Merl walked in.

"Something happened to Blackie! He has blood on his face, and he's acting completely crazy…!"

"He got hit by an airplane," Merl said.

We had a grass landing strip in the field back of our barn.

"What?"

"Yeah, I got into the plane to go for a ride with Bob, and Blackie came up to the door and wanted to get in. I told him to go back, and he headed up to the house. But I had my seat belt caught in the door, and when I opened it to free the belt, he must have thought I'd changed my mind, because he ran back through the propeller, just as Bob was starting it. It whacked him, and he turned and snapped at it as it picked up speed. I was sure he was dead."

"What?"

"Well yeah, I mean no dog is going to live through getting hit in the head by a propeller, so I told Bob I'd take care of him when we got back!"

"What?"

Merl went out to the barn to find Blackie, and to take him to be patched up. His unearthly cries had finally ceased.

By morning, he was eating and underfoot again, but as the days went by, and his face healed, we noticed a change in him. Always sloppily happy to greet company before, now he became suspicious and hostile. When he met the dry cleaner route man with bared teeth and wouldn't let him on the porch, I knew we had a serious problem on our hands.

In a short time, he extended his territorial protection to the road, not chasing cars for fun, as so many dogs do, but angrily challenging their right to use the highway. Always instantly obedient to any of the family, now he no longer would pay the slightest attention to us when we tried to call him back, or tried to still his snarls at visitors. He wasn't deaf, but he seemed to be obsessed by the demons that were driving him. Back on the tether he went, where he raged at each car that drove by or drove in.

"If I thought he ever had a brain, I'd say he has been brain-damaged," observed Merl.

The girls and I glared at him. We were speaking to him again, but he was treading on very thin ice.

We still took Blackie with us on the outings he loved, but

he was subdued and fidgety. Then one day, as we released him, ignoring our shouts, he roared out to the road to order a truck away, and landed on the lawn with a shattered shoulder. Knowing we were only prolonging the inevitable, we took him to the vet's and brought him back in a cast.

In a few days, he had broken the cast and was again raging at everything that moved. Sadly, we decided it would be best to have him humanely put to death, before he attacked a child on a bike or caused an accident.

"He really wasn't Blackie any more, was he, Mom?" said Diane.

No, he wasn't Blackie any more.

A FRIEND INDEED

Merl says what happened was my fault, because I told Charlie and Delbert not to go over Blue Hill dam in a canoe.

"You should have known they'd do it, if you told them not to!"

I don't accept any responsibility.

It was a nice April weekend, and the White River was still running high with snow melt, when our friends Del and Chas asked to borrow our canoe for a run down the river. We got it out of winter storage, along with the paddles, and the life jackets. The life jackets they dismissed. Charlie was wearing his favorite fisherman's cap.

"What section are you are you going to do?" I asked.

"We're going to put in up where the Third Branch comes in at Bethel village."

"Well, don't go over Bethel dam!" I said. "You'd lose your hat!"

"Never!" said Chas.

I meant it. I had put in right below the dam last year with my brother and, even though the center of the dam was broken out, it was nothing to try, with or without high water.

The canoe came back intact, but minus the paddles. It took a while to get the whole story.

They put in at Bethel village. A half-mile or so below the town, the brick powerhouse appeared, and they could hear the roar at the old dam. In the center of the structure, a section was broken out, and the whole volume of the river poured through that gap. It looked like a thrilling smooth ride to the big swirling pool below. It was, until they hit the huge chunk of broken concrete at the bottom. Then the ride became a bit too thrilling. The front of the canoe struck the block solidly, and the rear lifted and somersaulted, catapulting Charlie nearly across the pool. A couple of strokes with the current and Chas could touch bottom, so he made it quickly to the beach. Del wasn't so lucky. From his position in the bow, he was dashed into the icy churning water directly below the dam.

They weren't too coherent on how Delbert escaped. Something about luck and the current carrying him to the side of the pool, instead of downriver … and he was hypothermic by the time they got him to safety. They were both well aware that they had almost lost him and were sobered by the thought.

"And I didn't lose my hat!"

"Well then," I said brightly, "you're all ready to try another run next weekend!"

"I don't think so," he said.

Charlie did get back into our canoe at high water another time, though.

Having Chas around turned nearly any problem or catastrophe into a lark and we called on him for entertainment value as much as for his help. He came down the autumn day we had to bring the herd of dry cows and heifers across the railroad track to the barn. Animals that aren't accustomed to the tracks are usually very averse to crossing them, and these were no exception. We pushed and bullied them one by one to get them over and across the railroad, anxious to be done before a train came through. By the time they were all safely on the barn side of the road, they had scattered over the big field behind the barn. I got the car, and we went down to round them up. I dropped Merl off at one point and he started a group of them barnward, then left Charlie farther on. His weren't so cooperative and some high-tailed by him, headed south. I swung the car back to pick him up and he hopped onto the fender. I protested, but he was adamant, so I dutifully drove down to head them off. As I started to make the turn around them, Chas hopped off. I had no time to alter my course; the hind tire ran over the end of his toes.

Sometime later, I went into the garage where Charlie was head mechanic. Chas was curled up under the hood of a car he was working on, while the owners of the car—a couple I didn't know—stood by, watching and waiting.

I approached and addressed his back. "Is this the gentleman I have to see to get an appointment to fix my car?" I asked tentatively.

Charlie exploded out from under the hood. "Yeah! Come to me when you need help!" he shouted, "And then you run me over with your car!"

The poor couple looked on with stricken expressions. I faced them.

"It was just his foot," I explained.

In spite of his mishaps with us, Charlie was Johnny-on-the-spot the spring day the heifer ended up on the river island in flood time.

We were leading fall calves out to the shed across from the farmhouse, where they could become accustomed to the outdoors in the pen there, before we put them out to pasture. We had led a group of them over without incident and then brought the next batch. One of the first bunch was just hightailing up the railroad track.

Merl set out after her and I ran for the car. I pulled up just as the heifer ran across the road, knees lifting high and head in the air. She had been barn raised, so was very awkward in her movements. She ran across the narrow flat beside the road, and then went airborne as she ran off the steep bank. She tumbled to the bottom then continued on a bee line across the small strip of field below. Again she ran right into space, legs still churning, as she reached the river bank. She dropped nearly thirty feet into the roiling water, came up swimming, and struck out in the same direction, coming to the bank of the island well below where she had entered the river. She scrambled up the bank, and stood there, heaving.

Merl called Charlie at work.

"Want to go canoeing again?" he asked, and explained the problem. Charlie was there soon after quitting time.

Merl doesn't swim, but he put on a life jacket and gamely got into the canoe with Chas, well above the island. The current was running high and swiftly, but they disembarked on the island, and captured the heifer. I drove back to the farm, picked up a long stout rope and lugged it down to the river behind the barn. Charlie brought the canoe and I handed him one end of the rope. He paddled back and they attached it to the heifer's halter. I pulled, they pushed, and she came back into the water ... and didn't come up! She would have drowned if I had kept pulling. I let up on the rope, and she bobbed to the surface. She swam as I gently drew her to my side of the river. Merl and Chas paddled over and Merl led her back to the barn. She was shivering, terrified, and cold. She put her head under Merl's arm and pushed as close to him as she could all the way to the warm barn.

And we loved Charlie's tales of his misadventures, proving we weren't the whole reason for his bad luck.

Once, he had been scouting for deer sign for weeks before

deer season and had found the site and routine of a beautifully antlered buck. He could hardly wait for the first day of season. He was all ready to head out the door when he got a call from a hunter about his green Chevy station wagon that was broken down on Broad Brook Road. Disappointed, Chas went down to the garage and got out the wrecker.

He arrived at the car—and it was locked. No sign of the owner. Annoyed, but resourceful, Charlie got down under it and disconnected the drive shaft so he could tow it back to the garage.

Back home, ready to go out the door and the telephone rang. It was the state police. Seems they had a report of a stolen car on Broad Brook Road, and someone had seen Charlie towing it off.

Back to the garage, back to Broad Brook, drop the car, reconnect the driveshaft, then farther on up the road to pick up the correct car!

Finally, finally, he was in the woods, creeping up to the spot where he knew he would spot the buck when it came out to feed.

Another hunter was dressing out the buck.

One winter day he had been called out with the wrecker to retrieve a car that had skidded on black ice south of the village, landing on the ice of the White River. Chas winched it safely back onto the road and, incredibly, it was undamaged. As he climbed back into the wrecker to make out the bill, the city driver got into his car and set off with smoking tires for Massachusetts.

"He was making good time until he came to the end of the cable," Charlie said.

The man came back and sheepishly asked Chas how much he owed him. "Well," said Charlie, "it was going to be ten dollars, but now it's twenty.

TRAILING HORSES

My grandchildren are never sure whether their Grandma is pulling their legs with her tales of adventure in her long ago and far away life, but they listen eagerly anyway. And it really is easier nowadays to talk about what I did back then than it is to enact new story material.

Back in my checkered past, I had a children's summer farm camp. Since horseback riding was a big part of the program, I had nearly 30 horses and ponies. Most of my city-bred camp children had never been on or even touched a pony, so the first week or so of camp was a hectic time of acquainting them with the care of their mounts and the rudiments of riding.

Merl made me a crude wooden "horse" the approximate height and length of a pony, that I used to teach the kids to saddle and bridle; to mount properly; and how to use legs, weight, and reins to control their ponies. While it saved a lot of unintentional abuse of the ponies by well-meaning, but inept would-be riders, it took its toll on me. I usually could speak in only a hoarse whisper by the end of the first week.

The campers took to riding, for the most part, like country kids and, with a few notable exceptions, were competent enough in a couple of weeks to look forward to entering a junior western seat horse show and gymkhana … especially the gymkhana. Fortunately for me, my two older daughters, who were the same age of the campers, were available every day to straighten out the ponies who were confused by the kids' training, or which were all too willing to take advantage of the campers' lack of skill.

We chose horse shows that were at a distance of a day or two of riding. We sometimes had to camp out overnight on the way to and from the event. One of the shows was in Barnard, about fifteen miles from home. We rode over easily in one day.

The day of the show was hot and by the time it finished in late afternoon, the children were so tired that we fed and watered the horses and left them there. With supper finished and the kids off to bed with the counselors, Merl, friend Charlie, our oldest daughter, Terry, and I were driven back to Barnard by Chas's wife.

There we saddled up, then (I don't remember whose bright idea it was … probably mine) we each tied the halter rope of a horse or pony to the tail of our own mount, another one to the next horse's tail, and so on until we each had a string of horses behind us, finally setting off over the hills to South Royalton. It was a dark but pleasant warm August night, and we talked and laughed as we plodded toward home.

All went well for about an hour, until a terrific thunderstorm came up. The rain came down so hard it was like riding under a waterfall. We were drenched in moments. As we were being drenched, however, so were the tails and halter ropes. They soon parted company. As we slid off our horses to round up the loose horses, we dropped into water that was over our ankles. The narrow dirt road, up which we were riding, was now a raging torrent. We caught the horses and fiddled around with the ropes until we found a way to lead them beside us, and continue on our way. The rain was warm and none of us suffered any damage. We reached the farm without further incident.

After the next show, we brought the campers home to sleep overnight and took them back in the morning to ride the ponies home. Never let it be said that I'm not a quick study.

NEVER SPANK A PORCUPINE

I sat at the kitchen table, engrossed in the newspaper, and didn't really pay attention to the little porcupine squeaking at my feet. He had just had his breakfast and bath and I was letting him play a few minutes before he went back to his birdcage to sleep on the center perch for most of the day.

He shinnied up my jeans-clad leg and settled in my lap. I absently stroked him from his head back to his tail. He was just a baby. He grasped my hand and began to nurse on a knuckle. Still absorbed in what I was reading, I didn't notice as he became more frustrated at not finding milk. Suddenly he bit down hard with his little rodent teeth. I gasped and cuffed him beside the jaw.

My paper was immediately forgotten. I placed him, protesting, in his cage and went to get the tweezers to pull the tiny quills out of the back of my fingers.

So how had I come to the point where I could forget that a porcupine in my lap wasn't a mischievous puppy or kitten?

Maybe you had to be there.

Actually, it was a wonder that the little fellow ever lived at all, much more that he ended up in our kitchen, much less our hearts. I heard his story the day I stopped in at a friend's farmhouse up near Tunbridge. Piggy, a prickly ball not much bigger than my fist, was in a brass birdcage on the kitchen counter.

"Oh! Isn't he cute!"

"Wouldn't you like to have him?" asked my friend's daughter. She explained how he came to be there.

A day or two before, two young boys from South Royalton Village had shot his mother out of a tree. Then, seeing that the animal was very pregnant, they did an impromptu Caesarean section with a pocketknife. To their surprise, the little piglet came out alive and breathing.

Now, shooting an anonymous hedgehog was one thing. Killing this little miracle was quite another. They wrapped him up and carried him home. Their mother took one look and shouted:

"Get that thing out of my house! NO! You can't keep it!"

I was never sure how he ended up on my friend's kitchen counter, but they were looking for someone to take him…and I am such a soft touch for baby animals.

The girls were thrilled when I brought him home.

"Oh! Isn't he cute!"

Merl shook his head and went to the barn.

Our first problem was how to feed him. There was nothing in Morrison's Feed and Feeding about formula for orphan porcupines, so I mixed up some milk and corn syrup, and contrived a nipple from an old medicine dropper. He took to it greedily.

Next was the matter of personal hygiene. Porcupines don't have any, as anyone who has ever approached an old porcupine den can tell you. His cage was a smelly mess. How such a tiny creature could generate so much odiferous urine was amazing, but generate it he did. And tramp through it he did.

We drew an inch of soapy, tepid water in the sink and plopped Piggy into it. The first couple of times he shrieked and cried and scrabbled to escape.

"You'd think I was torturing him!" said Diane, as she grimly washed and disinfected the cage.

A day or two of protest was all it took. He decided that bath time was fun, after all. He jumped and spun and swatted with his tail. Week-ing with delight, he splattered anyone within reach. Soon he was protesting when we took him out.

Out of the tub and toweled off (he loved to have his tummy toweled) Piggy was ready to play. He waddled swiftly across the vinyl floor and up the first human leg he came to, squeaking happily as he attained the level of the table. Thwarted in climbing onto the table, he scrambled up to the shoulder. There he week-ed and wriggled, delighting in the attention he was getting.

He slept much of the day, but evening would find him sitting on the perch, front paws grasping the wires. Peering myopically through the bars, he'd week hopefully at anyone who came near. One of the girls always took pity on him and let him out. He loved to waddle from one to the other as they sat on the floor.

"Week! Week! Week!" he exulted, as he scrambled up their fronts to nuzzle under their chins.

"Man, his five o'clock shadow scratches!" Diane said.

As he grew he became more playful, pouncing at our feet, and then whirling as we stamped our feet at him. We were careful to keep our ankles out of reach of his little swatting tail.

The cat considered him of too low class to acknowledge and haughtily moved away whenever he approached her. However, though Smudge remained unruffled, the two beagles were completely undone by the little intruder.

Queenie had been introduced to a snoutful of quills in her youth, and she never forgot or forgave. After Piggy arrived, she slunk warily in to her food dish with raised hackles.

Poor Kissimmee was reduced to a trembling wreck. I had taken her with me on a solo backpack trek on the Long Trail the previous summer. The porcupines began to stir and to come close to camp at dusk, as I started my fire. Sim huddled against me, shivering and pushing. I finally unrolled my bedroll and opened the top for her. She dove to the foot of it, and there she stayed while I went back to cooking my supper. Having one of the scary beasts move into her house was really distressing. We petted and reassured both dogs and, in time, they tolerated having the little porc in the same room.

Then Piggy decided he needed playmates. Since the cat hissed balefully at him if he approached her directly, that left the dogs. It wasn't an easy sell.

He wooed them as winningly as he knew how. He was PORCUPINE! They backed off and bolted to the door to be let out. Piggy didn't give up. Day after day he waddled over to them, week-ing cheerfully, and tried to coax them to play. He pounced at them, landing with his chin on his front paws, his rump in the air.

At first, the beagles backed quickly away, then circled carefully and beat a retreat. Piggy kept up his campaign, jumping and spinning awkwardly, pouncing again and again, to land chin down, rump up. The dogs began to watch him, cocking their heads from side to side, puzzled by this friendly behavior of their enemy.

I was watching the day they finally succumbed. Piggy was at his most appealing, week-ing joyfully, spinning, pouncing toward the dogs. They couldn't resist the puppy-like antics. They both wriggled and wagged their tails. He pounced again and both dogs pounced back, chins on the paws—nose to nose with Piggy. In a flash, with every quill standing on end, he spun and smacked them both with his tail. They tumbled over backwards, yelping in pain and outrage. Piggy spun and jumped, week-ing gleefully.

It was two mournful, betrayed little dogs that submitted to having the quills pliered out of their tender noses. From then on, they circled the porc with bared teeth and warning snarls.

New visitors to our house did a double take.

"Oh! Watch out! He'll throw his quills! You'll get them in your eyes!"

I don't know anyone who believes that porcupines throw their quills that can be disabused of the notion. They gasped as I slipped my hand under his quill-less tummy and picked him up. Piggy nuzzled my chin and week-ed lovingly.

Others were intrigued. Those who gingerly petted him— from front to back—were amazed that they could do it without getting spiked. Piggy shinnied up any guest who would stand for it for a sociable chat. He became a popular figure in the neighborhood.

With his celebrity, came a nagging doubt about his future. It is unlawful in Vermont to keep a wild animal in captivity.

Porcupines aren't protected by closed hunting seasons. If they are at all numerous, they are very destructive of growing timber. In earlier years, there was a bounty on them. My brothers and I earned spending money when we were young, by bopping porkies on the nose and turning in their ears to the town clerk. That ten cents per pair of ears was a fortune to us when a candy bar or ice cream cone sold for five cents each.

It bothered me to think that we were breaking the law. I was sure that people obtained permits to keep animals in special circumstances, so I decided to find out how it was done.

No one could tell me. I called every agency I could think of in the state capitol of Montpelier. Yes, it's illegal to keep a wild animal. No, porcupines aren't protected. I don't know if a permit is necessary or not.

Piggy was soon going to be out-growing his cage and, with Diane and Lisa going back to school, he needed to be moved outside. We discussed how to fashion an outdoor wire cage, with a tree and warm sleep-box in it for Piggy for the winter. We heated our house with a wood furnace, so we would have plenty of hardwood limbs to feed him. Then, the game warden showed up one night.

"I understand you have a porcupine here."

"Yes. I've been trying to get a permit to keep him. Do you know how I go about it?"

"No. It's illegal to keep a wild animal."

"Yeah, but porcupines aren't protected!"

Merl had come out to the first room with me and the girls flanked us, facing the man.

We explained how we came to have him.

"Can I see him?" he asked.

"Piggy!" I called, "Get yourself out here!"

"Week?" he inquired from the kitchen. Then "Week! Week! Week!" He came rolling out in his best imitation of a gallop.

"Come here, Trouble!" I said, scooping him up. He was beginning to be an armful. The officer recoiled and looked at him in distaste. Piggy nuzzled my chin.

"Week," he murmured happily.

"Well, it is still against the law."

"So, it's all right for us to kill him, but it's against the law to nurture him!"

"Well, yuh!"

I looked at Merl. We had agonized over every facet of the

situation. We were breaking the law and there was no way that we could afford to engage in an expensive exotic legal battle that would almost certainly go against us in the end. I could see the inevitable closing in and grasped at one straw.

"The Fish and Game Department has porcupines on display at fairs and conservation camp. Couldn't you keep him for that?"

"I guess we could do that."

And the state could abolish taxes, too. My shoulders slumped.

"Diane, would you please get the cardboard box in the hall?"

She turned abruptly, tears running down her cheeks. We put him gently into the box and the girls stroked him tearfully.

"Week?" he called anxiously as the cover was closed.

The warden went out the door with the box under his arm, his nose wrinkled in disgust.

I watched him go, regretting that I had ever brought the tiny fellow home. How unfair, to have his joyous little life end so cruelly. It was only later that we could take some comfort in knowing that we had made as good as we could the short life he had. And we knew that never again would we look at a porcupine as just a stupid, slow destructive creature.

Lisa wasn't old enough to join in our philosophical musings.

"Mommy, they'll take good care of him, won't they?"

Merl and I looked at each other over her head, tears in our own eyes.

"He'll be all right, honey," I told her. "He knows we love him."

JAPANESE BEETLE INSPECTORS AND OTHER PESTS

If anyone had challenged me to name every category of agricultural inspector in Vermont, I would have taken him up on it. And I would have lost. There was one kind I'd never heard of, and I wouldn't have guessed it. No way would I have guessed it.

That category drove into our yard one day just as I was sitting down to the noontime meal with Merl and my brother, Howard, who, once again, was helping us through haying season. I padded, barefoot and in shorts, to the screen door to meet him.

He was, he informed me in no-nonsense tones, a Federal Japanese Beetle Inspector, and he wanted to discuss transactions in which I had taken part.

"Well, my stars!" as my grandmother used to say. I wandered out onto the porch, a bit bemused, wondering if my ears were serving me properly.

"Have you been doing business with Shore Acres Landscaping of Salem, New Hampshire?" he asked sternly.

"I don't know any 'Shore Acres Landscaping'."

"Are you denying that you have sold ferns then?"

It dawned on me then, what this must be about. Every spring and fall, a couple of fellows in a pickup truck bearing New Hampshire license plates, stop by to ask permission to dig dormant ostrich fern roots, which grow profusely in the woods down by the river. I don't know how much the ferns are worth, and never cared to find out. It's five or ten bucks we didn't have to sweat for, and if someone can make an easy dollar once in a while, more power to him, even if it's at our expense.

I sat down on the top step, suddenly overwhelmed by the momentousness of this occasion. Elbows on my knees, I rested my chin in my hands and looked up through my eyebrows at the inspector.

"Are you talking about those guys who come in here to dig ostrich ferns?"

"Don't you know that you have to have an inspection certificate to transport across state lines?"

"I'm not transporting ferns anywhere. I don't know what those guys are doing with them. They could be cooking and eating them at the first highway rest area, for all I know."

"This is serious!" he said. "There are federal regulations regarding the transporting of Japanese beetles across state lines!"

"Serious," I said, sitting up straight. "You could be right. What is this all about? Are you afraid that our Vermont beetles will crossbreed with New Hampshire beetles and produce a bigger better hybrid? Or, wait a minute! Are you implying that our Vermont beetles aren't good enough for New Hampshire beetles? Is this government-sponsored discrimination against Vermont beetles?"

Merl had followed me to the door. I could see him with my super-trained peripheral vision, anxiously signaling me to put a lid on it. Howard was peering from behind his shoulder, grinning broadly. I ignored them both.

The inspector pouted indignantly. He pointed a shaking finger at me.

"You are going to be in big trouble!" he shouted. "If you don't apply for a permit, you're going to be in big trouble! This is not a laughing matter!"

"No, I'm not," I said.

"You're not?"

"No, I'm not," I said firmly.

I stood up so I could look him straight in the eye.

"If I have to put up with this nonsense, then those guys can just go to—get their ferns somewhere else! And so can you!"

Merl could stand it no longer. Whether he couldn't bear the anguished prospect of my being hauled off to Leavenworth, or the thought of losing his chief—and cheapest—hired hand, I wasn't sure.

He stepped out the door.

"We haven't noticed any beetles around here this year," he said soothingly.

The inspector turned gratefully to him, relieved to have a rational person to talk to at last.

"Well," he said grumpily, "they'd be on your zinnias, if you have any. Do you have any zinnias?"

Merl eyed me with his sternest don't-you-dare look.

"Do we have any zinnias?" he asked, his voice rising in what I'm sure he hoped was a dire warning.

I stared back for a moment, weighing the temptation to send him out to the garden himself, just to watch him flounder in his ignorance of flora in general and annuals in particular.

Then I shrugged. My food was getting cold and besides, this poor old fellow wasn't really a worthy opponent. I could even muster a bit of sympathy for him. Going through life as a Japanese Beetle Inspector in Vermont can't be easy.

"C'mon," I said, "I'll show 'em to you."

There were no signs of the iridescent little pests in the flower bed and I sent him on his way shortly thereafter with his feathers no longer ruffled. And he hadn't, I noted with some satisfaction, given me any more warnings about trafficking in illicit ferns.

In November of that year, as I drove down Route 14 north of the village, I spotted that benighted old bugger again. He had a truck pulled over in a restaurant yard and was standing over an embattled farmer, who, his back stiff with outrage, was unloading, tree by tree, a large load of Christmas trees.

"Suck-er-r!" I chortled to myself.

You just have to know how to talk to those guys.

GUARD BIRD

We never put out bird feeders on our farm. As a number of reckless dive-bombing barn swallows could attest from Birdy Boot Hill, our barn cats were much too talented as hunters to give them the advantage of luring songbirds into the dooryard. We did buy a parakeet, though.

It soon became apparent that we hadn't given serious consideration to the problems inherent in bringing a bird into a household where one privileged cat had the run of the house as well as the barn. Furthermore, until Petie came to live with us I had no idea how many times a day the doors to the house were opened and closed.

No more: "Well, hello there! Come on in!"

It was now: "Wait! Don't open the door! The bird is out!"

He was a lovely little twitter of blue with a mind of his own. As soon as he became accustomed to us, he set out to train the family to his specifications. He seemed to know instinctively which wheel got the grease.

Smudge didn't stand a chance. She may have licked her lips a time or two when Petie first arrived, but she soon tired of being scolded whenever she came into the room. Petie learned in no time that loud pleading and scolding would prompt someone to come to his rescue, banish the poor cat to the porch, and let him out of his cage.

He drank from the dog's dish, ate Smudge's food. He strafed the beagles, who cringed and bared their teeth, but never snapped at him. He used the fishbowl for a birdbath.

He loved mealtimes, but he never acquired table manners that would allow him to stay for dinner. No one liked bird tracks in her mashed potato.

Putting him back in jail (after he had disgraced himself once again) brought on protests that ended only when one of us went out and threw a cover over his cage. That subdued him to indignant mutters, but had no beneficial effect on his future behavior.

He was back out of his cage one evening when we sat down to play BLITZ with the girls. Merl had just dealt the cards.

"Tweet?" Petie inquired, alighting on Diane's head. This looked like fun. He hopped down and promenaded around the draw pile in the center.

I drew another and he was back on board, eyeing the discard pile. I tossed a card down. Petie grasped it by the border, tugged it to the edge of the table, and dropped it off. He looked over the rim, cocking his head from side to side then, satisfied that he had disposed of it, strutted back to the center.

Merl and I were laughing, the girls were in stitches, and Petie tweetled with importance.

From that point, he became more industrious, trotting off with the discards, the draw pile, and the matches with which we kept score.

"Bombs away!" the girls cried as cards went over the side of the table, and Petie scurried back for more.

He allowed no interference with his game. If one of us

grabbed back a card from him, he flew to the hanging planter and furiously shredded my air fern.

Thereafter, if we wanted to really have a game with all the cards, or all the game pieces, Petie's parole had to be revoked. His unhappy murmurs from under his cover put a damper on our play.

More and more, Petie objected to being cooped up at all. I always let him loose for a while in the morning, after the cat was out and the door was securely closed. One day, however, while I was letting the cold water run to fill the coffee pot, Petie came swooping into the kitchen. I had made a practice of starting the coffee before I let him out of his cage, and this morning was no exception.

He made a couple of turns around the room before settling on the faucet arm. He danced up and down on it, chirping excitedly, as he eyed the running water, then hopped over on my thumb. I lowered him down, and he bent for a long drink, flipped the last drops over his shoulder, and took off, tweetling triumphantly.

I went out to the other room to see how he had gotten his door open. It was closed securely. He flew out and did a manic dance on the top of the cage. Completely puzzled, I returned to the kitchen. Petie carried on his usual dashes around the house, exulting in his freedom, returning periodically to perch on my head and noisily critique my preparation of bacon or muffin batter.

He always had breakfast with us, although it was a nuisance to keep him out of the hot coffee. Later that morning, I put him back in his cage, and there he stayed until he heard the water running the next morning. Then, just like magic, there he was again.

While we found his antics amusing, there were certain visitors who didn't appreciate Petie as we did. My mother in-law often dropped in at breakfast time and she definitely did not want a bird to alight on her head. We tried to shoo him away from her, but the little imp thought it was a wonderful game. He dive-bombed her each time like a demented bat, she ducked, and he would graze the top of her hair and swoop off, giggling evilly. So, in the interests of familial harmony I had taken to putting him back in his cage whenever I saw Mother coming up the walk, which worked fine until Petie turned into Houdini.

Still, no one had seen him escape from his cage and we couldn't figure out how he was doing it. He let his secret out because of his passion for piano music. He loved the piano and danced back and forth on his perch, singing lustily whenever one of us played it. If he was loose at the time, he would land on the keyboard and play jump rope with the player's fingers. Unfortunately for him, the piano was located in the same room as his cage.

I had started on a polka one night, Petie's particular weakness, when I realized that he had fallen suddenly silent. Turning, I saw him halfway out of his cage, a foot clasped on the upright wires on each side of him, shouldering his way through. He popped out, the wires resumed their shape, and he landed on my hand, whistling joyfully.

His inclination to mischief made him an unlikely ally for me one day in dealing with an unwanted salesman. How he knew that the encyclopedia salesman was terrified of birds I'll never know, but he set up an excited chatter the moment the man stepped into the room.

I didn't want any of his products. I didn't want to spend time convincing the salesman that I didn't want them, but I couldn't seem to push the fellow back through the door, nor shut him up.

He stood there, well into his spiel, while I faced him, hands on my hips, not allowing him one step away from the inside doormat.

Suddenly he paused, staring with alarm at something behind me.

"That bird is getting out!"

I looked. Sure enough, Petie was muscling his way to freedom. He flew over to perch on my head and gave the man a loud scolding. The poor fellow blanched, but gamely returned to his pitch.

Petie took a turn around the room then, screeching like a little blue banshee, he dove for the man's bald head. He didn't touch the first time, and swooped around the corner to the kitchen.

The fellow straightened up from his panicky crouch, and had just recovered enough to open his mouth again, when back came Petie on another run. This time he swooped lower, side-slipped almost into the man's face, then darted back around the corner. I could hear some very self-satisfied twitters.

The stricken salesman looked at me for help, but I was eyeing him benignly with a straight face, totally oblivious to his discomfort.

Back came my little Red Baron, and this time he ticked the top of that bald pate as he made his turn. The man threw one arm over his head and escaped out the door.

I sat down at the piano and played two polkas, just for Petie.

COW DOCTORING

I could tell that it was going to be one of those days the moment that cow sat in my lap.

I'm not at my most alert after a late evening, and I must have been sleepier than ever that morning because I hadn't noticed anything amiss as I put the milker on her stall mate. As I crouched to finish stripping the first cow, I felt Bessie crowding my back.

"Get over where you belong, you dumb hay bag," I said, backhanding her a slap on the belly.

I removed the teat cups and swiveled on my heels to dry massage Bessie's udder. She sighed softly and her hindquarters settled on my knees. I grabbed the milker pail and tipped it under her belly to catch some of her weight, but there I was, neatly trapped under a thousand pounds of paralyzed cow.

By then I was fully awake, but it was too late for clear thinking to do much good. I could just imagine the crunching and cracking of ligaments and joints if I managed to move my knees sideways. And no use in yelling - Merl was out of earshot in the sawdust bin. So I squatted painfully until he finally came wheeling around a load of sawdust.

"Would you mind rolling this cow off me," I asked

plaintively. "My other milkers are ready to be shifted."

He came sprinting to the scene and his concern was touching.

"Oh, the poor cuss! What happened to her?"

"How do I know, for cripes sake! Darn it! Will you get me out of here?"

He knelt down in the gutter and put his shoulder to her hip, still puzzling over her condition. I scrambled free, retrieved the milker, and he lowered her down again. We set the other milking machines on the back walk and began to check her over.

Ankles, back and ears cold; eyes dull; hindquarters paralyzed...classic milk fever symptoms. The only hitch in the diagnosis was that it had been nearly four months since she had calved and she was not a particularly productive cow. Milk fever occurs most often in high-producing cows that have just freshened. And she was grinding her teeth.

I limped up to the house to call Doc Roberts, and described the problem to him.

"Give her 500 of Dex-Cal," he said.

"You mean she has milk fever?"

"Well, I don't know if you could call it milk fever at this stage of the game, but it's a calcium deficiency and we treat it the same way."

"The beggar hasn't given milk enough to be deficient in calcium," I said.

Doc laughed and we hung up. I picked up the intravenous kit and a 5oo cc. bottle of Dex-Cal and headed back to the barn.

Back at the barn, I grabbed her nose and pulled her head around to expose the jugular vein in her neck. Merl inserted the needle and started the IV. We hadn't taken to warm the liquid as we usually did because her condition was so advanced. We just hoped that the cool liquid wouldn't put her into shock.

In a few short minutes, as the medicine went through her system, she came slowly back to life, and in fifteen minutes was back to normal and able to stand up again. If all medical conditions were so easily treatable and with such dramatic good results, I would have been a doctor.

Administering to cows with milk fever had not always been so convenient. For years we called Doc Roberts and he had to make the hasty trip over the hills from Woodstock to give the IVs. And it was not always as handy as having the cow safely in the barn.

Some years before, we brought the cows in late one afternoon on the rented farm where we got our start in dairying. One very pregnant heifer was missing. We set out to find her. It was soon apparent that she was not in the open fields that we were pasturing at the time, so we went through the fence into the woods, feeling desperate and knowing there was little chance that we would find her if she was in there. We wouldn't have, if she hadn't groaned. There she was, under a small hemlock tree, in the middle of calving, and down with milk fever. It was almost dark by that time.

I ran back to the house and made an urgent call to Doc Roberts. Fortunately for us, he was back from his rounds. He made the trip over the hill in jig time. That was the night that he told us that he was going to teach us to give an IV. He was as good as his word, and for some time thereafter we bought our IVs from him, administered the liquid and sterilized the equipment ourselves.

On another occasion I was alone in the barn in the early morning. It was a Saturday in deer hunting season and I had magnanimously offered to do the morning milking and chores so that my husband could go on the first drive with my father and brothers. I was to come along for breakfast and the second drive later. The gutter cleaner had worked splendidly, the cows were grained, and I was buzzing right along with the milking. I paused every so often to check Ruby in the maternity pen, where she was in the process of calving. I was nearly through with the milking when I noticed that things weren't going well with her.

I stepped into the pen and checked her over. All the symptoms of milk fever were there. I took the milkers off and ran up to the house to get the IV equipment. I was returning to the barn when my mother drove in to see if there were anything she could help me with. She followed me down to the stable. I fastened the bottle of calcium to the IV tube, twisted on the wide needle, pulled her head around, and inserted the needle into her neck. Rather, I tried to insert the needle. It was as dull as a hoe handle.

Again and again I tried, working up a sweat, becoming worried about the poor cow.

"Shouldn't you call the vet?" my mother asked anxiously.

"There isn't time now," I said, "She'd be dead by the time he could get here. I'll run up to the tool shed to get a whetstone."

I did, and quickly honed the needle to a fine edge. Not bothering to sterilize, I tried to insert the needle once more...success! Ruby soon began to come back to life, and not long after that she delivered a fine heifer calf.

I finished up my milking, washed up the milkers and the milkhouse, hayed the cows and heifers, and was ready to head up to Royalton Hill to join the hunters.

"Where have you been?" my husband demanded. "You don't have time to eat breakfast! We're all ready to head out now!"

All these years later, I still remember biting my tongue. Silence may be golden, but it sure gives me heartburn.

Doc Roberts was our veterinarian of choice, but once in a great while he was unavailable. This was the case one time when we were faced with a very sick cow. With some misgivings, we called a vet from another town-- who had to hire a young man to drive for him due to his accumulations of DUIs. Sure enough, he arrived well sloshed. Surprisingly though, he was still able to diagnose the problem in moments. Displaced Abomasums. Somehow, one of her "stomachs" had been twisted and she was in gross distress. The solution was to roll the cow completely over.

We stepped into place at his direction, the driver joining us; many dire warnings from the vet. As we started to roll the cow, she gave a frantic kick that would have taken his ear off, if it had be a quarter of an inch closer.

"See?!" he exclaimed, "I tol' you to be careful!"

The roll completed, we could see that the cow was much relieved. Her interior rumblings proved that the procedure was successful.

Although enabling us to give our own IVs took some stress off Doc Roberts, he couldn't shake everyone. He told us about one phone call that he received at 11:00 o'clock at night. He answered sleepily. A lady was on the other end.

"Could you neuter my cat sometime?" she asked.

"Couldn't this have waited until morning?"

His mornings usually began well before daylight. Unfortunately, some of his early calls required him to go through Woodstock Village. Woodstock is so precious that it has 25 mph speed limits for a long way before you enter the village. Doc's early morning treks through caught the interest of one of the town policemen, and he was there every morning to trail Doc from one end of the village to the other. Doc kept his speed to the posted limit until, one frosty morning, he had reached his limit. He spotted the patrolman tail-gating him, pulled over abruptly, hopped out of his Jeep, and stormed back to the cop's car.

"If you don't have anything better to do than harass me every day, then you'd better find something! I have to treat a cow in Reading that may die before I get there, and if she does, because you insist on slowing me down, I'll advise the farmer to sue you, and I'll testify for him!"

He strode back to the Jeep, put it in gear, and sped off through the empty streets of that "special" town at 40 miles per hour.

He chuckled with satisfaction as he told us about it.

"I haven't seen him since," he said.

FUTILE TAIL FLICKING

There's an old snippet of farm advice that, by and large, is pretty good counsel: "If you're going to eat it, don't name it." We usually regretted the times we ignored that advice.

We hadn't raised any pigs for several years. It had become difficult to find someone to slaughter and cut up hogs over time, and even harder to find someone to cure and smoke hams and bacon. That wasn't the only reason, however. We didn't get to eat the last two we raised.

Merl had brought the pair home. They were big enough to eat pig mash and the vegetable peelings and pods from my cooking and canning projects, but still small enough to be pink and white and cute. Terry, Diane, and Lisa immediately fell in love. Tommie and Tillie had found a home. The girls regaled me with the precious antics of their newfound pets.

"Now, look here!" I warned them. "You know we got those pigs to put in the freezer this fall. They aren't pets, they're meat! Don't go getting attached to them!"

Pigs have personality…and a lot more intelligence than other animals around the farm. It was going to be an uphill battle to turn those little porkers into Sunday dinner, I knew.

It brought to mind the fable of "HOW THE CHIPMUNK

GOT HIS STRIPES" from one of my childhood books.

The tree containing the chipmunk's family toppled over on the shore of the ocean. (I know chipmunks don't raise their young in trees, but squirrels don't have stripes, so don't argue with the fable!) As the tide came in, the frantic father sought to save them by dipping his tail in the surf and then flicking the water onto the sand in an attempt to lower the water level.

Dip, flick,—dip, flick, on and on he labored. Mother Nature came along and asked him what he was doing. Dip, flick, he—dip, flick—told her—dip, flick—the problem. Mother N waved one hand and washed the tree up onto the beach to safety. With the other she drew her fingers down his back, leaving shiny black stripes on his tawny little body.

"Henceforth," she said, "the chipmunk shall wear these stripes as a symbol of your devotion and faithfulness."

Dip, flick. Don't name those pigs! Dip, flick. Stop playing with those pigs! But I was dipping and flicking without the faith of Papa Chipmunk.

Came November and there was no point in thinking of eating T and T. Teary-eyed, the girls agreed to let them go to the weekly auction sale. At a loss. I was teary-eyed thinking of someone else eating my pork chops and bacon.

It was years later before I broached the subject again. We now had Tracy, who was seven; Lisa, who was twelve; and Terry and Diane had both married and had left the farm.

Merl and I discussed the matter at length. I felt it somewhat a point of honor to raise nearly everything we ate. We put a beef in one end of the meat freezer every autumn, and I raised fryer and broiler chickens, plus a few roasters, and we put the old hens in for stewing chicken when the new pullets started laying eggs. I even caught dace and suckers in the river and froze them to feed the barn cats. I wanted pork in there, too.

"If we have to buy pig feed, it would be cheaper to buy the

pork and put it in the freezer," he said.

"But the pork never gets bought! And I have a lot more scraps and vegetable peelings to feed them than my hens can take care of!"

I finally prevailed.

This time Merl didn't bring home little and cute. This one was four months old and well started. I was busy when he unloaded it. Lisa and Tracy helped put it in the pen. They brought its water and feeding of mash.

The pig ignored the feed, pushing up to the fence, grunting gently. Then it sat down beside the trough and looked steadily up at Merl. He reached down and scratched it behind the ears.

"Urf!" she said, and began to eat supper contentedly. Merl told me about it when he came in.

"Don't you dare name that pig!"

Darn déjà vu.

The next summer, with Merl's health failed, we sold our cattle and machinery to a young man and leased him our farm for five years. He had several sows, and raised piglets to sell. We gave him Susie.

He had a grand pig roast that fall, and invited all the neighbors. Susie was the guest of honor.

PATCHES

I was as horse crazy as any other ten-year-old girl. Utter bliss for me was the old pony my father brought home one summer day. My brothers were definitely not enamored of horses, so she was essentially my pony.

Two pony-owning friends and I spent three fun-filled years of bare-back riding, until my pony became too old to take part. I was entering high school by that time and other interests and responsibilities crowded in to take her place.

Patches came into my life one night in a small load of western horses we had ordered from a dealer for our children's summer camp. They arrived after dark, so we unloaded, stabled, fed, and watered the horses without really looking them over. Early the next morning, I was out there to see what we had acquired. There were three small horses that appeared to be gentle and mannerly; a skinny bay that towered over seventeen hands, that flattened his ears and bared his teeth at my approach; and there was Patches. She took my eye immediately.

Patches was a sturdy paint with an intelligent eye and an impressive deep arched neck. She watched me anxiously as I stepped up beside her, spoke to her, then stroked her as I untied her halter rope. She backed out readily and I took her out into the yard to look her over. She was well-marked, deep chestnut and white with a black mane and tail. I curried her. Her chest was wide and her back broad, her coat shiny, and her tail a little sparse. I saddled her easily, but she fought the bit as I raised the bridle to her head. I put it on, led her to the corral, and swung into the saddle.

She responded instantly to the slightest pressure of rein, leg or weight, and I put her through her paces. Her trot was the most tooth-jarring gait I'd ever encountered, her lope was a smooth as a rocking chair, and she changed lead in figure eights without prompting. I fell in love.

Tex and Barbara, the couple who were handling the horses and horsemanship program for us that summer, arrived early to look over the new horses. The campers, too, were all out of their bunks and up to the farmhouse from the camp in record time that morning. Everyone was finished with breakfast and cleanup chores and ready for horsemanship lessons at nine o'clock.

Tex decided that he had better try out each animal himself, so we saddled them and he gave each one a workout around the corral. The three small ones were just as gentle and mannerly as they had first appeared. The tall bay, we skipped. He was foul-tempered and much too tall for our novice youngsters.

Tex liked the appearance of Patches. She fought the bit once again and shook her head frantically after the bridle was on. Tex took her into the corral and mounted. He trotted her around the enclosure and I could see a distinct change in her manner from when I had ridden her. She was working herself up into a sweat, thrashing her head up and down, fighting the bit, and holding to a trot only under his hand. He put her into a canter, and again he had to fight to keep her under control. He pulled her in at the far end of the corral and walked her back to the gate. She was fairly dancing on the tips of her toes, her eyes rolling in distress or fright.

Tex brought her up to the gate where we were waiting, and the horse grew wilder and more agitated. I scattered campers just in time, as she reared and came crashing down on the gate, splintering the boards. Tex bailed off and I grabbed her bridle and pulled her down. I talked to her and stroked her neck, and she stood quivering with her head down against my arm.

"That horse is an outlaw!" Tex exclaimed. "She's not safe for anyone to ride!"

I scratched her well-padded withers, feeling the trembling beneath my fingers.

"Nobody touch this horse," I said. "I'm going to keep her for myself."

Bit by bit, Patches became my dream.

The first thing I wanted to determine was why she was so agitated about taking a bit in her mouth. Perhaps one of her teeth was bad. I examined her mouth and found that her tongue had been nearly severed where the bit crosses it. It was an old wound, completely healed, but I could only shudder at what that mare had been put through while she was being broke. I went up to the harness shop to talk with the old-timer. He brought out a bitless hackamore and I took it home to try it on her.

Patches objected to taking the hackamore just once. From then on, she was a different horse. No head tossing or fretting when I put it on or reined her in; we could move on to other things.

I discovered that Patches was schooled in working stock horse skills far beyond my elementary knowledge. The bull-dogging stop, for instance. Soon after she arrived, Merl and I, with our friends Charlie and Bunny, began to take evening trails rides now and then. Merl rode Sugarfoot, a black with one white sock; Bunny, a little buckskin named, naturally, Bucky; and Charlie adopted that towering, malevolent, ungainly bay, whom he christened Rebel. We had taken a leisurely ride up through the pasture and over the high hill overlooking the farmstead, and were returning up the road south of the corral. I pressed Patches into a lope, and the others, coming from behind, caught us at a gallop. Patches surged ahead and we were moving toward the horse barn much too fast. A hackamore isn't made to force a horse to stop. It will only control a well-trained one, and since I hadn't yet learned the leg/weight/rein combination she had been taught, hauling on the reins wasn't having any effect. She was streaking headlong toward the barn. Despairing of stopping her, ten feet before we hit the door I bailed off. At least I started to bail off. The second my weight hit the left stirrup, Patches set all four feet, her rump lowered almost to a sitting position, and we skidded to a halt. I dismounted as the others trotted up.

"Cutting things kind of close, weren't you?" asked Charlie.

I looked at the chunky little paint, standing placidly, her sides hardly heaving.

"I just found out she has power brakes," I said. "Hey, that's right! She has power steering and power brakes."

From then on, it was a joy to discover just how unique that little horse was. I was with my campers on a trail ride one morning and we were coming home through an abandoned pasture. My oldest daughter, Terry, was in the lead and she took her pony through a gap in an old stone wall, where the old wire fence had long since fallen and lay under years of grasses. One of the horses behind Terry caught a foot on the wire and pulled it out of the grass a bit as he went through. I sat on Patches at the side, waited for all the children to go through, and then moved her to the opening. She stepped carefully down through the fallen stones, lifting her feet high, and then her ankle came up against the wire. She froze in mid-step. I looked down and saw that she could easily step over it. I urged her on. She wouldn't budge, just hunkered there, quivering, on three legs, the other suspended against the wire. I dismounted, and tried to lead her forward. She balked. I grasped her foot, raised it over the wire, and set it ahead, then led her the rest of the way through the gap. I remounted, and she trotted happily after the others.

She was petrified of a wire or cable lying on the ground, whether because she thought they were snakes, or because she had been tangled in wire, I had no way of knowing. When we came upon a farmer's electric fence cable lying across a back road one day, I had to get off and coax her over it with great difficulty.

Riding through the hills on hot, humid summer days occasionally found the horses and ponies too overheated when we came to watering places. I grew hoarse constantly cautioning the children not to let their mounts drink more than a few swallows until they had cooled them down. Patches, whether from mustang heritage or some most unhorselike instinct, never had to be restrained from drinking too much. If the water were deep enough she would bury her face to the eyes and blow, and splash back and forth with relish, but she would only take a sip or two when she was lathered.

Patches didn't want any horse ahead of her. As long as she had the lead by a neck, she was satisfied and calm, so we rode point most of the time. That had a distinct advantage the night we ended up on the top of Johnson Hill at dusk and were galloping along the straight stretch of road at the top. Patches, in the lead as usual, jumped the skunk in the road without getting sprayed. The others were not so lucky.

That same quirk, however, got her into trouble one day when my daughter, Lisa, cantered up beside me on little Sundance. Patches, in one ill-tempered toss of her head, swept my tiny three-year-old cowgirl out of her saddle onto a hard-packed gravel road. Without even thinking, I swatted Patches hard right between the ears with the reins—the only time I ever struck her with anything. Lisa was skinned up a bit and heart-broken that Patches had "attacked" her, but back on her pony, she was soon her sunny self. Patches hung her head and pouted all the way home. She never again challenged with her head any horse that might be gaining on her, although she was determined to maintain the lead for the rest of her life.

She didn't grow any fonder of men. Our daughters, Terry and Diane, could ride her in the ring without any problem. Put a small child on her back and, with head bowed, she would docilely follow the youngster leading her like a patient dog. But men around her made her noticeably nervous, and when one showoff tried to ride her without my knowledge one day, she went completely to pieces again and demolished another corral gate. When I got out there, I cut short his tirade about what I should do with an "outlaw" like that with a terse, explicit description of what I would do to him if he ever touched my horse again without my permission.

I rode her in parades (bareback, if the camp kids were "Indians" for the occasion) and she arched her neck and danced to the music. We were a band of Indians convoying our "Burning of Royalton" float down Main Street in Bethel one Saturday morning, and had reached the center of the business block when a train went through. The tracks are directly behind the south side of the block, and the train whistle suddenly blasted with a deafening scream. Patches, on her toes and showing off, reared in fright, and I, as startled as she was, gripped her fat slippery sides with my legs, holding onto the reins for dear life. She came down immediately, but the yank on the hackamore had broken the nose piece, and here I was in the middle of a parade with just a flimsy collar around her neck. I put my hand against her neck to guide her back on course and we finished the parade with her chin tucked under, neck arched extravagantly, dancing sideways on her toes, down to the end of the street, then back up through the crowds lining the sidewalks in the business block, and out of town to the schoolyard where we had started. I doubt that three people in the crowd realized that my horse was almost completely on her own.

A few years later, finally pregnant with our fourth child, I decided to take the time to really enjoy this baby, so announced that this was the last year for Tegdum Farm Camp. Toward the end of the season, I advertised some horses for sale.

One prospective buyer, a gentleman with whom I'd had some public political differences, drove in to look at them without an appointment. I took him to the back of the dooryard where we could look down on the night pasture.

"That black one with the white foot is for sale, the buckskin, the little black and white paint, the gray, and the small bay," I said, pointing them out.

Patches immediately took his eye.

"What about that one?"

"She isn't a kid's horse, and she isn't for sale anyway. She's my horse."

"Well, what would you take for her?"

"She's not for sale."

"I'll bring my daughter down to try them out Saturday. Have the black, the little paint, the buckskin, and that paint ready."

I nodded, annoyed at his attitude, but needing to move some horses.

On Saturday morning, I must have been feeling a bit perverse because I brought Patches up to the corral and saddled her up with the others. He drove in with his teenaged daughter as promised. He wouldn't even look at any horse but Patches.

"She doesn't want anyone to ride her but me. She isn't a kid's horse, and she isn't for sale."

"Get on and try her out," he told his daughter. The girl got on and took her once around the corral. Patches was nervous, but behaved herself.

"I don't like her," said the girl, as she slid off.

"I'm going to try her out," he said.

"She's not for sale, and she doesn't like men."

He mounted, and Patches' eyes rolled. He took her around the corral at a walk, and she fretted on tiptoe the whole way. He could apparently sense that she was wound up because, as he was approaching the end where we stood watching, he yelled to his daughter:

"Open the gate!"

"I wouldn't do that," I said.

They ignored me, and he swept through the gate and headed down the road. He was out of sight when someone called me from the house that I was wanted on the phone. I trotted over and took care of that. The daughter was on the porch looking anxiously down the road for her father when I came out. I walked with her to the spot overlooking the pasture, and talked with her about the ponies and horses below. At last we heard Patches' hoof beats. We went to the middle of the dooryard where we could see the knoll where they would appear. She came over the rise, running flat out. He was hauling on the reins.

Up across the railroad tracks, up the paved road. Instead of reining her toward the corral, he turned her across the lawn toward us. She didn't slow a bit as she veered. Right by us, straight toward the front of the house they flew. At the very last instant, faced with sure destruction, he decided to abandon ship. The second his weight hit the left stirrup, Patches went into her famous roping skid, neck arched, chin in, rump tucked under, and Super Jockey did a perfect swan dive right over her head into my big rambling rosebush.

In a lifetime one may experience only a few perfect moments. This was one of mine. I stood surveying the lovely river view to the east as he disentangled himself from my roses, cursing wildly.

"That (bleep) horse is a killer! She ought to be shot! She isn't safe to have around."

Patches eyed him benignly, now that he was off her back and I was holding her hackamore. I eyed him thoughtfully, too, discarding the retorts that came immediately to mind.

I swung into her saddle.

"I said she isn't a kid's horse," I said mildly, and she turned smartly around for me, and trotted calmly over to the corral.

He bought the docile buckskin.

BACK ROAD DRIVING

"I'd better teach you to drive before we get married," said my fiancé. "I won't have the patience to do it afterwards."

There should have been a warning bell tolling there somewhere, but I didn't hear it.

My driving lessons were a bit unorthodox. I spent a lot of time that summer of our engagement, helping Merl with haying. This was 1950 and mobile hay balers in our area were still a couple of years in the future. Hay was mowed, allowed to dry in the swath, raked into windrows, then loaded onto the wagon with a hay loader that was pulled along behind the wagon. One person (me) drove the tractor, and Merl skillfully forked and placed the hay on the load so that it wouldn't slide off on the way to the barn. There my truck driving lessons began.

The hay was put into the large hay mows in the barn with the use of a "hay fork", a kind of oversized tongs. This device traveled on a track the length of the barn, and was raised and lowered by means of a heavy "hay rope" attached to the bumper of the new one-ton International truck, Merl's pride and joy. What made it a real challenge was that I had to raise each "bite" of hay by backing the truck, and not just backing, but a torturous process that involved inching backward to tighten the rope, then backing at the precise nerve-racking speed required to make the fork operate correctly, and stopping the instant Merl yelled, or risk smashing the whole apparatus. The tension kept my asthma in full bloom, but I doggedly wheezed my way through the routine again and again, day after day.

I managed fairly well at the barn on the home farm, but then we went down to hay the Dutton farm, which Merl rented. Here I had to back down over a small rise, through a narrow gate! I had done it many times without incident--not counting the times I didn't keep the speed consistent, to Merl's impatient annoyance—and had to pull ahead to dump the bite on the load, then start over. And over.

Then came the day my brothers and some of their friends were "helping". They were in the back of the truck, yelling instructions. I was backing through the gate, trying to listen for Merl's shouted "Whoa!!!" I turned the wheel just a bit too soon and heard the sickening crunch of shiny red fender meeting gatepost. I stopped and waited as Merl strode down, looking like a thundercloud. He examined the damage.

"Did you do that?" he demanded.

That has to be one of the dumber questions of all time, so I did what any normal person would do. I laughed. That nearly ended a promising engagement.

The summer passed. In August, a vengeful former brother-in-law torched Merl's barn on the home farm. We moved our wedding date up from the following spring to September, and I became a permanent farmhand. We began a routine that was to continue for years as Merl took off-farm employment. While Merl secured winter lodging for the herd (they were in the night pasture, thank goodness, when the barn burned) and built a temporary milking shed, I did much of the last hay cutting and raking, fall plowing and harrowing, and manure spreading.

To this day, although I'm right-handed, I still drive the car with my left, a legacy from all the hours and years of steering with my left, while operating equipment levers with my right. And my dreams of becoming a pilot were thwarted years later, when upon taking lessons, I realized that the throttle on an airplane works exactly opposite from the way the throttle on every tractor I'd ever run did. I could just imagine myself in an emergency situation, automatically pulling the throttle back to give the plane full power, and having the engine shut down on me because I was supposed to push it!

"I'll have to have a jack put on the throttle," I told Merl, "if I'm going to fly."

Mother Nature took care of my problem by somersaulting our club plane down the field at Barre City Airport one day, when a windstorm came up. Some employee had moved it and neglected to tie it down. By the time the insurance company came through with the settlement, the flying club had disbanded and I never pursued flying again.

My pre-wedding road driving lessons were just as out of the ordinary as the barnyard truck-driving lessons. The truck had a four-speed stick transmission, in the day when synchro-mesh (automatic) transmissions were still reserved for a few luxury sedans. This one had to be double clutched. In those days before seat belts, I rode in the center of the big bench seat, cuddled up to Merl as he drove and, since his right arm was around my shoulders, he would engage the clutch, I'd shift to neutral, he'd rev the engine, then I shifted up to the next gear as he engaged the clutch again. It was a delicate, sometimes noisy, dance, and I created a few new gears before I got the hang of it.

I did learn to drive well, although it was several years before I bothered to get a license and I have little patience with people nowadays who don't know how to drive silly little cars with manual transmissions.

In the meantime, we had moved from Merl's home farm up

onto a hill farm that was reached by narrow dirt roads, with some hills steep enough that down-shifting in motion was required. That took even more practice, as did the slippery, icy, or muddy surfaces of winter and spring.

As I gained more experience, I learned the nuances of back road etiquette.

On a road too narrow for two cars to meet in the middle of a hill, the one coming up has to back down...especially in winter. (I expect these common sense rules harked back to horse-and-buggy days.) First car on a narrow bridge has the right of way, next one has to wait. Car coming into an intersection on the right has the right of way. When meeting on a narrow road, wait to see if the other car gets by without getting stuck. If not, stop and help him out of the ditch.

This rule got stretched to the breaking point for my Dad ' one time.

When I was a child, there were quite a few "summer people" who had bought Vermont hill farms and spent their vacations on them. It was about that time that a few decided it would be a good idea to stay on year around. They didn't bring country driving skills with them. One fellow in particular, who lived about a mile west of us, never did get the hang of winter driving. Invariably, when one of his neighbors met him, Frank would plow off into the ditch and bury his car in the snow bank, then get out and dither about uselessly as the neighbor dug him out. Often, he would just be waiting in his ditched car for someone to come along to do his digging for him. My Dad, a rural letter carrier, and his farmer friend and neighbor, Den, were getting more and more annoyed with the novice, particularly since he didn't carry a shovel in his car, and they would seldom go to town or back without meeting him or finding him stuck somewhere on the way. They finally decided on a way to teach him to carry a shovel, and how to use it.

Dad came off his route one winter day from the opposite direction from town. We were curious, but he wouldn't tell us why he was taking such a round-about way home. And Den no longer came over the road by our house, either. This went on for a week or so, and then we learned what was going on. This city fellow drove by one day just after Dad came in.

"Well, wonder if Frank has his shovel with him today," Dad said.

A neighbor who lived down the hill from us told Dad what had occurred in the past few days.

The flat near their farm nearly always had snowdrifts across the road. They were hard-packed and difficult to negotiate with a car. Needless to say, our hapless city neighbor had no such driving skills, and he hit the ditch when he tried to cross the drifts, whether he was meeting another car or not. He had done it the first day of Dad's revolt. Ray was chuckling when he reported to Dad.

"Frank hung around waiting and waiting for someone to come along to do his digging. I saw Albert come up my hill in his log truck and spot him up on the flat, and he turned right around in my driveway and went back the way he come! Finally, Frank decides nobody is going to come along, and he comes trudging down to my place.

"'I'm stuck in the ditch up there,' he says when he come in.

"'So I see,' I says.

"He fidgeted around a while, and then he asked me if I have a shovel he could borrow.

"'Yep, right on the porch', I says, not making a move out of my chair by the stove. He was a sorry sight, dragging that shovel back to his car. Took him all afternoon to get it out. He don't shovel no better than he drives!"

His driving didn't improve, but he did begin to carry his own shovel. Sometimes Dad or Den stopped to help him out of the ditch after that, and sometimes they just raised a finger in genial greeting and drove right around him.

The finger raise was standard form in the ritual of back road greeting. It had nuances that might not be apparent to the casual observer and was governed, for the most part, by how well you knew the person you were meeting; on how well you liked him; or sometimes, on what sort of mood you were in when you left home. In general, with both hands on the steering wheel, the salutes were as follows:

1) First finger raised...I see you and I greet you, in case you know me.

2) Two fingers raised...Hello, I know you.

3) No finger raise, but head tipped back, and mouth open wide in silent greeting....Hi, there!

4) Two fingers raised, head tip-back, and mouth wide in silent greeting...Hi, there! Good to see you, friend!

5) Hand off wheel, enthusiastic, big grin...Glad to see you, friend! (Farm woman driver.)

6) No finger raise, no head tip, no open mouth, no wave...city driver in Vermont.

Since those early days I have logged thousands of hours on tractors, in pickups and cars, have covered a good portion of the country and driven in a good many cities in the U.S. and Canada. I have a rule that works for negotiating an unfamiliar city, or any city, for that matter, which I imparted to my youngest daughter when she had her student license, and when she wanted me to drive when we reached the outskirts of Salt Lake City.

"Tracy," I told her, "don't ever sweat missing a turn. Two wrongs don't make a right, but three left hand turns do."

It has stood her in good stead ever since, and it hasn't let me down yet.

WALK A MILE IN MY BARN BOOTS

For the last time, no, I was not trying to barbeque my husband in a grass fire. If I had been trying, for Pete's sake, would I have given him a hundred foot head start?

I suppose I could spout scripture, the way a neighbor does when she is backed into a corner. Matthew 1:7 would be appropriate right here. Or I could quote that Indian admonition to walk a mile in my moccasins before I throw stones at your glass house or something, but I don't want to appear defensive. I'll just explain what goes on around our place and then I don't want to hear another word about how mean I am to Merl.

We were putting in baled hay. Merl was driving the tractor, which pulled the wagon in which I was taking my turn stacking bales as they were brought up onto it by an ingenious conveyor device. I had placed the last layer at the top of the sideboards.

There were only a few dozen bales left in the field however, so he ignored me and continued to pick them up.

It was a struggle, but I wrestled them up, higher and higher, finally stowing the last one precariously on the top. Merl stopped the tractor, unhitched the bale loader, and then hopped back on and headed us toward the barn. I was not particularly well pleased to be riding on top of that swaying load up around the steep driveway to the barn, but I didn't have a choice at that point. Once in the dooryard, and turned to back into the barn floor, it became apparent that the load was two tiers too high to fit through the doorway. I waited, with jaw set, to see if he would back in anyway, just to see me scramble, but he shut off the motor and climbed down.

For me, climbing down was another matter. With the bales piled far above the sideboards, the only handholds I would have were the unstable bales themselves. Jumping onto that hard driveway with my gimpy knees was out of the question.

"Hon, give me a hand, will you?" I said.

"Sure," he replied, holding up his hand.

I dug my sneakered heels into a bale below me as best I could and bent way down to reach his hand.

And then he gave a yank.

"You said 'give me a hand,' didn't you?" he said, as he ran for the protection of the house. "I gave you a hand!"

But my temper that day didn't approach the feverish high of one certain afternoon with our infamous 24T International baler.

I have long had a theory, confirmed many times by close observation, that civil engineers and mechanical engineers who finish in the lowest ten per cent of their classes (and I suspect, manage to graduate only by having the answers to final exams cribbed on their shirt cuffs) are hired exclusively to design highways and farm machinery, respectively. It is the only explanation I can find for the fact that I-89 has a northbound lane in Royalton, Vermont, that runs due south, and that farm machinery is designed with every working part located in the most inaccessible position it is possible to devise on every piece of equipment.

That miserable baler was certainly no exception. It was one

of the first string-tie models, and the knotter was a constant source of annoyance. On the small rolling fields that we often worked, there were many turns and tight places. Nothing could be more frustrating, negotiating a particularly troublesome corner without shearing a universal joint pin on the power take-off shaft, than to find, strung out behind me, all the hay I had just put through the baler in untidy little pats of broken bales.

Frustrating as the knotters were however, at least they were up on top of the machine where I could clean and adjust them with a minimum of lost knuckle skin. The shear pin on the fly wheel of that beggar was something else.

The flywheel was located inside of the front of the bale chamber and changing a sheared pin required me to lay on the ground to remove the remaining piece, then crawl out and stand on my head to try to determine the hole alignment. That done, the real fun began: aligning the holes so I could replace the pin. There was no way of turning the flywheel by hand, ensconced as it was in its cozy little nook in the bale chamber. The only thing to do was to set the tractor brakes, hope they'd hold, put the tractor in neutral (this was before the day of live power takeoff), get out a huge Stillson wrench, and yarn on the power take-off shaft. Then stand on my head and down on my back to view those elusive holes. Then try again. And again. Never could I accomplish it in less than forty-five minutes, though heaven knows I tried.

With two people it was much easier. One could eye the holes as the flywheel was turned by the other, and guide the turning, and insert the new pin, when the alignment was made.

This day, we had a lot of hay down and ready to bale, so Merl hired a neighbor's boy to help him to put it in, while I baled the hay. I was on a small river flat when they drove in to pick up the bales around the perimeter of it. This meant that I wouldn't have to get off to move bales all around the field before I could bale the final back swath. I really appreciated the assistance.

My gratitude was soon forgotten.

Careful as I was to avoid wads of hay that might overtax the finicky machine, nevertheless I heard the dreaded snap of the shear pin. The flywheel spun fruitlessly as I stopped the tractor, put it in neutral, set the brakes and stepped down. Pulling the wrench from the toolbox, I went back and crawled under the baler. The men were nearly done with their first load, but they were on the farther end of the field. They would be coming by me when they drove out. I readied the power takeoff and tried to determine how far off the hole alignment was, while I waited for Merl to come up to help me put the pin in.

They drove slowly up the field, waved merrily to me, and drove right by! They didn't even offer me some of the lemonade in the jug I had put in the front of the truck that morning. It is hard to align a shearpin hole when you are viewing the world through a purple haze of fury.

So when people shook their heads reprovingly and told me that they were sorry for Merl, after we burned the roadside down below our place the other day, I didn't have much patience. Where were they when this other stuff was going on?

It came about this way. The banks beside the half mile of road bordering our main field are too steep to reach to the top with our mowing machine without overturning the tractor, so we find it necessary to cut the brush by hand every two or three years, and then burn the built up grass and weeds to clear the bank and keep it neat. We had our fire permit from the local warden and a fairly windless day in which to attend to that chore.

Merl took a five gallon can filled with gasoline to the foot of the bank nearest to the barn and, since what breeze that was stirring that day was coming from the north, away from the buildings, he began to drizzle a stream of gas along the base of the bank. About two hundred feet down the line he turned the nozzle up, stepped aside, and shouted for me to touch it off.

I obligingly tossed a match onto the spot where he had started the gasoline stream. The flame pouffed to life then snaked leisurely down the line in enchanting little puffs and starts until it reached the spot where Merl stood. He had set the gas can aside, and we watched the fire as it cleaned the bank of the dry debris, while we stomped out little errant licks of back fire.

That section burned over, we moved on to repeat the procedure on the next. I watched the progress of my little conflagration with interest, gauging the timing carefully. The next time, I waited until Merl was half way through his gasoline run, and struck my match.

"Don't stop!" I called to him.

Merl looked over his shoulder to see why I was yelling, and a look of panic came over his face. He made a few running steps, then tipped the can up and jumped aside.

"Don't you do that again!" he shouted angrily.

It hadn't even come close. I could do better than that.

We continued down the field, me testing my timing perceptions, Merl running, skipping, jumping, threatening, being reduced to a nervous wreck. He was one tired puppy by the time we finished. Meanwhile, a long parade of neighbors and passers-by had stopped to view the proceedings with interest and varying reactions, some of them being pity for Merl.

So I have just one thing to say to my concerned neighbors: you try yanking me off a load of hay, and see what I do to you!

NOTE TO TODAY'S GENERATION:

My lovely granddaughter, Aubree, who has been assisting her technologically challenged grandmother with formatting her manuscript, has two requests for me. She desires me to explain what a telephone "party line" was, and to describe the Blitz game we played in the Guard Bird chapter.

Back when I was a kid, a private telephone was expensive and rare. Instead, the party line had a string of rural neighbors on one line. If everyone on the line picked up their receiver earpieces at one time, they could have carried on a neighborhood conservation…if the overloaded batteries permitted. The lowest number of party customers on one line that I knew of was four, a luxury, I'm sure. The largest was 13.

To make a call, we turned the ringer handle on the right side of the wall phone…one long ring to get the operator to assist with a long distance call, or turning the handle the appropriate long and/or short rings to call an on-line neighbor.

If everyone was respectful and considerate, it worked quite well. That was not always the case, however.

Years later, after I married, our party line served considerate neighbors for quite a while. Then another party, (from an adjoining town, no less) was added to it, and we found ourselves unable to find the line open for hours at a time. That additional neighbor was a non-stop talker, and she didn't take a hint that someone needed the line when they picked up the receiver. Nor did she pay any attention to "ahems" or tappings. My husband reached his limited limit of patience when he rushed in from the barn one morning to call the veterinarian for a very sick cow. Our favorite yacker was on the line. Nothing made her hang up, including a polite request to let him call the vet.

He stormed up to his parents' house and called the vet. Then he called the telephone company, described the situation on our line, and let them know that they could give us a private line, or remove our service altogether.

We had a private line in jig time.

Personally, I suspect that it was the complaints of her neighbors on her previous line that inflicted her on us and our neighbors.

Now the Blitz game. Three pennies were counted out for each player. The deck was shuffled, three cards dealt out to each player, and then placed in the center of the table with one card turned up beside it. The object of the game was to reach "31," meaning an ace and two face cards of the same suit.

The first player could pick up the up-turned card, if it fit his hand, or draw from the pack. This continued around the table until someone had "31," when losing players put a penny in the center of the table. When a player had lost all 3 pennies, he was out of the game. This continued until all the pennies were paid into the pot, with the last winner "winning" the pot.

The pennies always went back into the game box when we finished playing, because actually winning money in a game changes the whole nature of the game, even if the winnings are only twelve cents.

ABOUT THE AUTHOR

   Phyllis Tenney Mudgett once sent a letter to the governor of Vermont, offering her body to be stuffed, mounted, and displayed beside "The Last Vermont Panther" in the Vermont History Museum, as a representative of a rapidly disappearing species: a native-born Vermont farmwife. She grew up on a tiny farm in the hills of Vermont surrounded with brothers, male cousins, and rowdy neighbor boys. She held her own. This book covers a part of her eventful life. Phyllis has spent eight decades using her wry wit and ready tongue and pen to create memories worth sharing with the rest of us. A lifetime of experiencing life to its fullest and always discovering a new adventure now finds her in the midst of yet another one in the wilds of Florida, where she lives with her husband, Merl.

no farm growing up, her dad was a mailman, 2 younger brothers, no other boys within a mile, one cousin her same age

Made in the USA
Lexington, KY
30 January 2015